Playwrights on Playwriting

Other Anthologies edited by Toby Cole

Acting: A Handbook of the Stanislavsky Method
Actors on Acting (with Helen Krich Chinoy)
Directing the Play (with Helen Krich Chinoy)

Playwrights on Playwriting

THE MEANING AND MAKING OF MODERN
DRAMA FROM IBSEN TO IONESCO

Edited by TOBY COLE
Introduction by JOHN GASSNER

A DRAMABOOK
HILL AND WANG • NEW YORK
A DIVISION OF FARRAR, STRAUS AND GIROUX

For Aron and Johnny
who helped the most

FIRST DRAMABOOK EDITION AUGUST 1961

12 13 14 15 16

Library of Congress Catalog Card Number: 60–7642

Manufactured in the United States of America
by the Colonial Press

PREFACE

MODERN DRAMATISTS have freely exercised the privilege of fame to express their views of life on both sides of the theatre's curtain. A book drawn from these comments would be many times the size of this one; but its contribution to our topic would be peripheral. A surprisingly smaller group of playwrights have addressed themselves centrally to the art and craft of playwriting. They are represented here.

Most of the acknowledged masters are present. But great gift in playwriting is not always accompanied by acuity in formulating dramatic theory. In some instances we encounter major statements by playwrights whose plays were not equal to their precepts. Zola's naturalist manifesto reminds us that innovators are sometimes outdistanced by followers who benefit by the formers' extension of dramatic form when, as Strindberg says, "the new wine has burst the old bottles."

Part I, *Credos and Concepts,* with its fervent expressions of artistic conviction, its battle cries and proclamations, reflects the modern dramatist's restless search for form toward and away from realism. The marvelous ways in which these abstractions have been substantiated in many of the finest plays of the period comprise Part 2, *Creations.* It is my hope that this ordering of the materials documents the way in which dramatists have animated this era's ideas of the theatre. It should be noted, with particular reference to Part 2, that dates given after the titles represent the year in which the selection was written, rather than the time of composition or production of the plays discussed.

My task was singularly favored in aim and scope by the personal encouragement and aid of two of our finest scholar-critics: Eric Bentley, Brander Matthews Professor of Dramatic Literature at Columbia University, and John Gassner, Sterling Professor of Playwriting and Dramatic Literature at Yale University. I am deeply grateful to them both.

Robert Corrigan, editor of the *Tulane Drama Review,*

generously gave me first call on the *Review*'s valuable Documents Series. From this source came Strindberg's "On Modern Drama and Modern Theatre," and essays by Toller and Duerrenmatt translated by Børge Gedsø Madsen, Marketa Goetz, and Dr. Gerhard Nellhaus, respectively.

I should like to express my appreciation to Joseph M. Bernstein for his valuable counsel on editorial matters as well as his translations of Giraudoux, Cocteau, and García Lorca.

Thanks are due to Evert Sprinchorn of Vassar College who brought to my attention and translated the Ibsen Notes on *Hedda Gabler,* and corrected other items from the Danish and Norwegian; to Samuel Draper for a new rendering of Zola's "Naturalism on the Stage"; to John Willett for the first publication rights to his translation of Brecht's "A Short Organum for the Theatre"; to Eric Bentley, once again, for his selection from Hebbel's *Journals* and contributions to Brecht's "Organum."

Kind consent for the use of material was given by Francisco García Lorca, Jean-Pierre Giraudoux, Mrs. Eugene O'Neill, Jean Cocteau, Eugene Ionesco, and various publishers who are acknowledged throughout the volume.

Finally, in a personal vein, I want to thank my sister-in-law, Helen Krich Chinoy of the Smith College Theatre Department.

TOBY COLE

CONTENTS

PART 2 Creations

EUGENE O'NEILL

JEAN COCTEAU

SEAN O'CASEY

T. S. ELIOT

ARTHUR MILLER

TENNESSEE WILLIAMS

EUGENE IONESCO

INTRODUCTION

(1)

IT IS no secret to anyone familiar with the theatre that modern playwrights have been a self-conscious breed. Anyone whose wares are so conspicuously on display and make such excellent targets for critical marksmanship is bound to be self-conscious. Modern playwriting, moreover, came into being during the latter half of the nineteenth century when intellectual conflict was making itself felt in the theatre and writers were even becoming oracular. Old dispensations in the arts were being challenged; new dispensations were being explained and defended. The age of literary criticism was moving toward high noon. Critics were becoming playwrights, play producers, or stage directors; and it followed that the playwright could turn critic if the critic could turn playwright. Imbued with new intellectualism and estheticism, showmanship itself—once a simple, if not indeed simple-minded, activity—began to buzz with theories supplied by scenic artists such as Appia and Craig and directors such as Antoine and Stanislavsky. Objectives were constantly affirmed or revised in a theatrical world from which improvisation and intellectual innocence had departed while ideas and ideologies multiplied. The modern theatre, it would seem, was born with a program, and it will probably end with one.

From the abundant literature on the modern drama written by the playwrights themselves Toby Cole has compiled a volume rich in matter and provocative in manner. To read the discourse of intelligent writers on their principles and problems is to observe the modern drama in the making. We merely allow for the fact that there is always a breach between ambition and attainment, and especially so in an art so utterly dependent upon stage production and the intervention of the actor. The danger of succumbing to "the intentional fallacy" need not deter us from attending to the playwrights' objectives once it is understood that we shall judge the play

rather than the authors' intentions. It is not likely, moreover, that their pronouncements will make bigoted converts of us and limit our horizons or so bewilder us
with their variety as to make us incapable of judgment.
We live in an eclectic age, are unlikely to be seduced
into exclusive dramatic theory, and have been inured to
contradictions.

Fortunately, too, the playwrights afford a relatively
simple perspective. We find them engaged to two kinds
of theatre—the *modern* and the *modernistic*. The first
sought realism of content, style, and form; the second
aspired toward poetic and imaginative art. The first began
to expel romantic and pseudorealistic drama from the
theatre by the 1870's, the second to challenge, modify,
and supplant realism by the 1890's. But romantic drama
was never conclusively routed by the realists, and realistic
drama has not been substantially displaced by neoromanti-
cists, symbolists, expressionists, and other proponents of
poetic or imaginative drama. Styles of dramatic composition have jostled each other and contracted marriages
throughout our century.

It is surely true, besides, that realism is as much a
"style" as any nonrealistic fashion of playwriting. Style
in the latter case is merely so conspicuous as to give an
impression of stylization, whereas style in realism is con-
cealed to such a degree as to afford the illusion of naturalness. We are concerned with theatrical reality whether
we erect or banish an imaginary "fourth wall" between
the actor and the audience. The realists endeavored to
make the theatre less theatrical after it had been meretri-
ciously "theatricalized," while their usually younger opponents, the antirealists, wanted to make the theatre
more theatrical after it had been "de-theatricalized." The
culprits in the first instance had been mediocre romanti-
cists *and* show-business operators; the culprits in the
second instance, mediocre realists *and* show-business
operators. Whether distinguished playwrights spoke for
or against realism, then, they were equally aiming for
distinguished theatre.

It does not of course follow that they were invariably
successful, or that they were superior to error in their
respective procedures. Scientism trapped naturalists and
partiality for the commonplace mired realists, while an
overfondness for subjectivity made symbolists turn poetry

into mist and expressionists transform dreams into night-mares. It follows only that we do not have to take ir-reversible sides in an ideological war when different play-wrights offer conflicting opinions or programs. The play-wrights themselves set us an example: Maeterlinck, for instance, acclaims Ibsen as a great symbolist writer while Shaw honors him as the supreme dramatist of ideas. Synge avows himself the enemy of Ibsen and Zola whereas he could have convincingly contended that he was making it possible for creative realism to thrive in Ireland. O'Neill is at one point convinced that naturalism is in-solvent but is not deterred from composing naturalistic tragedy in *Desire Under the Elms* or from bringing his latter-day career to a climax with *The Iceman Cometh* and *Long Day's Journey Into Night*. Most of the im-portant modern playwrights, from Ibsen and Strindberg to O'Neill and O'Casey, did not actually make exclusive commitments to any philosophy or style of theatre, al-though they sometimes wrote as if they were making them.

In reading *Playwrights on Playwriting* it is well to realize that the authors' most fervent generalizations usually proclaim a departure from convention that may no longer seem necessary or urgent. To appreciate the force of their pronouncements we should possess some knowledge of the practices they rejected; or else we should be capable of imaginatively identifying these practices, which current malpractice or the insidious re-turn of discredited practices (humdrum realism, preten-tious symbolism, or morbid expressionism) will make dis-couragingly easy. Thus Shaw had a certain vapid kind of contrived playwriting in mind when he struck at "Sardoodledom," and Strindberg was not tilting at a paper dragon when he fought for multidimensional characterization. In his polemical essays he had in mind the nineteenth-century practice, present alike in Bouci-cault's plays and Dickens' fiction, of reducing the in-dividual to a type and the type to a trait; character-draw-ing became caricature. We must realize the extent of the provocation when Strindberg declares that "a character on the stage came to signify a gentleman who was fixed and finished—nothing was required but some bodily de-fect—a club foot, a wooden leg, a red nose. . . ."

It should be apparent that the playwrights speak to

us most effectively when they have in view the problems and principles with which they were involved as *creators* rather than as theoreticians. We turn to their essays for an introduction to their collective and individual aims and practices. We must agree with Brooks Atkinson when he reminds us that "rules are only a by-product of creation, which is the sole business of art." It is not in search of "rules" that we seek out a playwright's commentary. We still want to read it because it may cast some light on his personal effort and achievement, as well as because it may rouse us from the torpor of standardized expectations and responses. It is not absolute principle, for example, but stimulation (including the stimulation of dissent) that we derive from Bernard Shaw's declaration that "A play with a discussion is a modern play; a play with only an emotional situation is an old-fashioned one."

It is evident, too, that the effectiveness of a prescription depends partly on the patient. Shaw could safely assume that old-fashioned playwrights would not write discussion plays, but he must have known better than any of his readers that a discussion play would be dull if written by a dullard and old-fashioned if written by an old-fashioned thinker, or by no thinker at all but a Philistine—however new-fangled the chatter that constitutes the outer garment of his thought. Conversely, it is also possible to be distinctly "modern" while discoursing not at all skeptically on such "old-fashioned" matters as morality and manners —when the discourse, let us say, is by Lionel Trilling rather than by Bruce Barton or some publicist of "positive living." It may also happen that the prescription does wonders for the patient at one time and very little for him at another; "discussion drama" yielded *Man and Superman* at one time and *Fanny's First Play* at another. We cannot escape the conclusion that playwrights writing on playwriting are worth heeding in so far as they are provocative and suggestive rather than prescriptive.

It is not even certain that they always know exactly what they have accomplished or that they accomplished what they intended—it is even possible for a writer to have deviated into something remarkable by *missing* his predetermined target. But it does not follow either that a playwright's understanding or even misunderstanding of his work is without significance. That Chekhov thought he had written *The Cherry Orchard* as a "comedy" is important to our understanding of the play, particularly in a translation, even if we should be convinced—and grateful (as I am)—that he did not. Shaw's prefaces are gratifying and revealing even when they bear only a faint relation to the play they introduce. They may represent the mental climate in which the play came to life—and the mental climate is a significant quality of Shavian playwriting.

In the case of a specific program, indeed, the direct result may matter less than the indirect. Yeats, for example, dreamed of furthering the cause of poetic drama in establishing the Irish national theatre, but there was only one Yeats in Ireland. He got noteworthy drama from his colleagues of the Abbey Theatre almost exclusively in prose plays of peasant life such as Synge's *Riders to the Sea* and *The Playboy of the Western World*. He wanted, above all, *romantic* drama from the Irish theatre; even Maeterlinck was not romantic enough for him. He did get the somewhat unfinished *Deirdre of the Sorrows* from Synge in 1910, but it was not romanticism drawn from the glorious Celtic past but a clamorous realism wrung out of the inglorious present that saved his declining Abbey Theatre when O'Casey rescued it with *Juno and the Paycock* and *The Plough and the Stars*. Nevertheless, Yeats found and fostered "poetic drama," too, in the very realism of the young O'Casey; the paradoxes of creation never cease. It is a paradox, too, that when, after 1917, Yeats came to the peak of his personal effort to create poetic drama, he wrote not for his Irish national theatre but for private drawing-room performances and took for his model not a native but an exotic, Japanese form of drama.

The case of Maurice Maeterlinck is equally instructive. When the Belgian symbolist wrote his celebrated essay on *The Tragic in Daily Life* in 1896 he proposed plotless, static drama as the ideal form for the modern theatre, and his program won considerable support. Subsequently he revised his eloquently expressed views, revoked them indeed as a youthful extravagance (in a letter to the late Barrett Clark), and wrote "active," more or less melodramatic, plays. Nevertheless Miss Cole exercised exemplary judgment in reprinting the essay in which he advocated "static drama." He was at the height of his

powers as a playwright when he wrote this apologia, and
it defended his practice in such poetic one-acters as *The
Intruder, Interior,* and *The Blind* which won the ad-
miration of the modern theatre's arch-realist, the great
Stanislavsky, himself. Synge's related practice in the virtually plotless *Riders to the Sea,* produced in Dublin eight
years after Maeterlinck's essay, resulted in the greatest
one-act tragedy in the English language. Maeterlinck had
his finger on the pulse of modern drama in expressing a
widely felt dissatisfaction with plotty playwriting which
resulted in attacks on the "well-made play" from such
different schools of writing as those represented by
Strindberg, Shaw, Yeats (in the very same essay in which
he asserts romantic ideals), and Andreyev, who pro-
claimed—I should say, rather prematurely—that life in
the modern world had moved inward. For better or
worse, plot and external action did lose status in the
modern drama, as they did, more thoroughly, in fiction. The
Zolaist naturalistic "slice of life," the Shavian discussion-
play, subjective and psychological drama—these and other
types of dramatic writing have reflected the same tendency. Well-regarded plays such as *The Glass Menagerie*
and Carson McCullers' *Member of the Wedding* (as well
as present-day avant-garde works by Beckett, Ionesco,
and others) continue to exemplify the vitality of a principle Maeterlinck laid down, too romantically and dog-
matically yet by no means absurdly, more than half a
century before.

(2)

In one respect or another, then, the effort to create
a modern theatre receives support and personal interpretation from every playwright represented in the present
collection. The strivings for such a theatre have been
manifold, and it is risky to predicate unity in diversity
for the main pursuit of modern dramatic theory and
practice. One would have to allow too many exceptions
to the rule for the rule to have any validity. But para-
mount in the modern experiments and achievements is
the determination to express some aspect of reality, some
measure of experience, some vision or conviction. This
is the organizing principle of Ibsen's work when he develops modern realism and of Brecht's when the latter
promulgates his antinaturalistic "epic realism"; and it

appears alike in the social optimism of Shaw's and O'Casey's plays and the nihilism of Beckett's and Ionesco's.

The search for truth of experience comes into view when Ibsen declares as early as 1874 that "All that I have written these last ten years I have lived through spiritually"; it reappears when Zola declares: "I am waiting for someone to rid us of fictitious characters, of these symbols of virtue and vice which have no worth as human data. . . . I am waiting for everyone to throw out the tricks of the trade, the contrived formulas, the tears and superficial laughs." The errors of Zola-sponsored naturalism have been aired often enough; they need not discredit the ambition to give dimension to character, a degree of meaningful determinacy to behavior, and fluidity to dramatic action. Nor is Strindberg to be ignored when he makes a necessary distinction between microscopic or "little" naturalism that sees only the minutiae of reality and the naturalism that provides the wide prospect of, let us say, Hauptmann's *The Weavers* rather than the same author's *Lonely Lives* or *Before Sunrise,* with its doctrinaire genetics and small-souled sociology.

Nothing perhaps corrects false perspectives better than Strindberg's distinctions, set down in 1889 and still indispensable to theatre, in the great essay "On Modern Drama and Modern Theatre" Miss Cole has so ably edited for inclusion in *Playwrights on Playwriting.* On one hand, we find in the theatre "the little art that does not see the forest for the trees," the "misunderstood naturalism" that photographs everything but actually reveals nothing. On the other hand, we have the possibility of *"the great naturalism"* (that of *The Power of Darkness* and *The Plough and the Stars,* for example) which, Strindberg says, seeks out "the great battles" and takes delight in the conflict of powerful human forces. And Strindberg adds the one requirement least likely to occur to the "little naturalists"—he expects playwrights to see reality through a *temperament.* When he rejects a reflection of life devoid of temperament as inadequate because "soulless" he does something momentous, whether he does so knowingly or unknowingly; he invites not only passion but poetry into the modern theatre. Once these are present in a play, along with what Strindberg calls "significant motif," the differences between realistic and imaginative, naturalistic and poetic drama become technical and, in the main, superficial.

Once this is understood, we do not have to feel that we are either pushed back from the modern theatre or thrust out of it whenever the poets and the advocates of "the theatre theatrical" speak their piece. We are moving in the right direction of the expressive dramatist rather than the juggler when Maeterlinck asks the playwright to deal with an essential life "beyond the life of every day" and calls for an "atmosphere of the soul" in the theatre, although we may well prefer Chekhov's "atmosphere" to Maeterlinck's. We can appreciate Maeterlinck's point when, in calling for "sorcery" in the drama, he finds "sorcery" in *The Master Builder,* even if we suspect pinchbeck mysticism when he writes such puerile sentences as "It is this sorcery that imposes action or the power of the beyond. And we have to yield to it. Whether we want to or not." We can also agree with Yeats and Synge when they want the theatre to be rich in language. "On the stage we must have reality, and we must have joy," Synge's famous sentence in the preface to *The Playboy of the Western World,* does not order playwrights to leap out of time and space by means of mystical rocketry. Synge, whose beautiful dialogue comes from the Irish peasantry, is not so far removed as we might expect from John Galsworthy, the confirmed naturalist of the English stage. In "Some Platitudes Concerning Drama" Galsworthy praises *The Playboy of the Western World* for its natural matching of matter and poetic style. He objects only to an "ill-mating of forms" (in plays, I take it, where verbal poetry and the subject matter are at odds) and warns that the poetry in ordinary naturalistic drama "can only be that of perfect rightness of proportion, rhythm, shape—the poetry, in fact, that lies in all vital things."

In this brief introduction it is impossible to dwell upon the various ways in which modern playwrights have tried to make the best of the two possible worlds of "reality" and "poetry," or endeavored to treat them as identical or interchangeable. But it is also true of course that a number of modern playwrights (Yeats, Lorca, Giraudoux, and Ionesco—to mention just a few) have, at one time or another, proposed imaginative flights that would whisk us out of the orbit of everyday life. I do not believe that they have usually realized their program without botching their plays or even at times "realizing" themselves right out of the theatre. It would appear, too, that the reality of everyday life often seeped right back into their more or less successful plays. Giraudoux's characters are often piquantly mundane in the midst of the fantastic and supernatural action of such plays as *Amphitryon 38, Intermezzo,* and *Ondine.* Cocteau's return to the Oedipus legend in *The Infernal Machine* is spiced with many an intentionally anachronistic detail more native to the Parisian boulevard theatres than to the classic theatre of austere tragic vision.

In spite of these qualifications, however, it is gratifying to observe that the flight of the modernistic playwright has often been *into the theatre*—where all good playwrights belong—rather than into the blue inane. This has been evident in the practice of Giraudoux, Anouilh, Ionesco, Wilder, and other twentieth-century playwrights. The necessity of landing in the theatre was understood by them all, as their comments show. Moreover, their "flight into the theatre"—that is, the "theatricalization" or distinctly theatrical realization of the subject matter of the play—could actually result in an intensification and highlighting of reality, as in Brecht's *Mother Courage* and Wilder's *The Skin of Our Teeth.* It became certain in our time that the "theatre theatrical" did not necessarily conflict with the playwright's engagement to modern life. He could use the theatre as show-window, pillory, or rostrum as, for instance, Brecht did in different plays. These and other expressive uses of the theatre have been widely recognized by contemporary playwrights; and at least in its best practice, the modernists' flight from illusionism into imaginative theatricality has advanced, rather than retarded, the contemporary theatre.

How well contemporary reality is presented or projected, how soundly appraised, how conclusively judged —these questions must, of course, receive answers that will fit the individual case. Fortunately Miss Cole has devoted the second part of her compilation to notations by playwrights on the specific plays they have written— from *A Doll's House* in 1879 to Ionesco's *The Bald Soprano* and *The Chairs* in our own time. These essays, which are concerned with individual creation, are illuminating in themselves, and they are instructive when read in conjunction with the plays to which they pertain. They take us into the creator's workshop. The notes are not offered as a passport to the heart of the mystery of creation, and they cannot of course take the place of the final work, which will probably differ from the author's best-laid original plans. The insights afforded by the notes are, nevertheless, important additions to the *Credos and Concepts* of the first section of the book, exemplifying or confirming them, fixing them in a specific context, and perhaps, when read in conjunction with the play itself, illustrating the difference between the aim and the fulfilment. In all respects, then, *Playwrights on Playwriting* is an important theatrical and literary document; and more than that, it is a collection of opinion and data that should have practical value to playwrights in our time and in the foreseeable future. Looking into this book, we may not be able to tell which grain of an idea or principle will grow, but we have much to choose from in the data Toby Cole and her publishers have so generously made available.

JOHN GASSNER

PART 1 Credos and Concepts

HENRIK IBSEN
(1828-1906)

The Task of the Poet[1] (1874)

... AND WHAT does it mean, then, to be a poet? It was a long time before I realized that to be a poet means essentially to see, but mark well, to see in such a way that whatever is seen is perceived by the audience just as the poet saw it. But only what has been lived through can be seen in that way and accepted in that way. And the secret of modern literature lies precisely in this matter of experiences that are lived through. All that I have written these last ten years, I have lived through spiritually. But no poet lives through anything in isolation. What he lives through all of his countrymen live through with him. If that were not so, what would bridge the gap between the producing and the receiving minds?

And what is it, then, that I have lived through and that has inspired me? The range has been large. In part I have been inspired by something which only rarely and only in my best moments has stirred vividly within me as something great and beautiful. I have been inspired by that which, so to speak, has stood higher than my everyday self, and I have been inspired by this because I wanted to confront it and make it part of myself.

But I have also been inspired by the opposite, by what appears on introspection as the dregs and sediment of one's own nature. Writing has in this case been to me like a bath from which I have risen feeling cleaner, healthier, and freer. Yes, gentlemen, nobody can picture poetically anything for which he himself has not to a certain degree and at least at times served as a model. And who is the man among us who has not now and then felt and recog-

[1] Henrik Ibsen: "Speech to the Norwegian Students, September 10, 1874," *Speeches and New Letters,* translated by Arne Kildal (Boston. Richard G. Badger, 1910), pp. 49–52. After an absence of ten years, Ibsen spent a couple of months in Norway during the summer of 1874. On September 10, Norwegian students marched in procession to Ibsen's home. This speech is Ibsen's reply to their greeting.

nized within himself a contradiction between word and deed, between will and duty, between life and theory in general? Or who is there among us who has not, at least at times, been egoistically sufficient unto himself, and half unconsciously, half in good faith, sought to extenuate his conduct both to others and to himself?

I believe that in saying all this to you, to the students, my remarks have found exactly the right audience. You will understand them as they are meant to be understood. For a student has essentially the same task as the poet: to make clear to himself, and thereby to others, the temporal and eternal questions which are astir in the age and in the community to which he belongs.

In this respect I dare to say of myself that I have endeavored to be a good student during my stay abroad. A poet is by nature farsighted. Never have I seen my homeland and the true life of my homeland so fully, so clearly, and at such close range, as I did in my absence when I was far away from it.

And now, my dear countrymen, in conclusion a few words which are also related to something I have lived through. When Emperor Julian stands at the end of his career, and everything collapses around him, there is nothing which makes him so despondent as the thought that all he has gained was this: to be remembered by cool and clear heads with respectful appreciation, while his opponents live on, rich in the love of warm, living hearts. This thought was the result of much that I had lived through; it had its origin in a question that I had sometimes asked myself, down there in my solitude. Now the young people of Norway have come to me here tonight and given me my answer in word and song, have given me my answer more warmly and clearly than I had ever expected to hear it. I shall take this answer with me as the richest reward of my visit with my countrymen at home, and it is my hope and my belief that what I experience tonight will be an experience to "live through" which will sometime be reflected in a work of mine. And if this happens, if sometime I shall send such a book home, then I ask that the students receive it as a handshake and a thanks for this meeting. I ask you to receive it as the ones who had a share in the making of it.

Translation revised by Evert Sprinchorn

ÉMILE ZOLA
(1840-1902)

Naturalism on the Stage[1] (1881)

THE IMPULSE of the century is toward naturalism. Today this force, racing toward us, is being emphasized more and more, and everything must obey it. This force has abducted the novel and the drama. The development of the naturalistic force has progressed more quickly in the novel to the point of triumph; on the stage it is just beginning to appear. This was bound to be. The theatre has always been a stronghold of convention for many reasons which I want to explain later. I would like to come simply to this point: the naturalistic formula, however complete and defined in the novel, is far from being well stated in the theatre, and I conclude that the formula must be realized and that it will take on a strictness of form emanating from its scientific nature, or else the drama will become blunted and more and more inferior.

Some people are very angry with me, and they shout, "But what do you want? What further development do you need? Is this evolution not already an accomplished fact? Have not Émile Augier, Dumas *fils*, and Victorien Sardou pushed as far as possible the observation and the painting of our society? Let us stop at this point—we are already too concerned with the realities of this world." First of all, these people are naïve to want to stop this naturalistic development; nothing is stable in society, everything is carried along by sustained motion. People go, nevertheless, where they ought to go. The naturalistic evolution, I contend, far from being an accomplished fact, has hardly begun. Up to now we have experienced only the first attempts. We should wait until certain ideas have made their mark, and until the public becomes accustomed to these ideas and until their force destroys the obstacles one by one. I have attempted in looking over Sardou, Dumas *fils*, and Augier to explain for what reasons I consider them workmen who are clearing the ground of rubbish,

[1] Émile Zola, "Le Naturalisme au théâtre," *Le Roman expérimental* (Paris: E. Fasquelle, 1902).

and not as creators, not geniuses who are building a monument. Moreover, after them, I am waiting for something else.

This something else which arouses indignation and calls forth so much jesting is, however, very simple. We have only to read Balzac, Flaubert, and the Goncourts again —in a word, the naturalistic novelists—to find out what it is. I am waiting for someone to put a man of flesh and bones on the stage, taken from reality, scientifically analyzed, and described without one lie. I am waiting for someone to rid us of fictitious characters, of these symbols of virtue and vice which have no worth as human data. I am waiting for environment to determine the characters and the characters to act according to the logic of facts combined with logic of their own disposition. I am waiting for the time when there is no prestidigitation of any kind, no more waving of the magic wand, changing persons and things from one minute to the next. I am waiting for the time when no one will tell us any more unbelievable stories, when no one will any longer spoil the effects of true observations by imposing romantic incidents, the result of which destroys even the good parts of a play.

I am waiting for everyone to throw out the tricks of the trade, the contrived formulas, the tears and superficial laughs. I am waiting for a dramatic work void of declamations, majestic speech, and noble sentiments, to have the unimpeachable morality of truth and to teach us the frightening lesson of sincere investigation. I am waiting, finally, until the development of naturalism already achieved in the novel takes over the stage, until the playwrights return to the source of science and modern arts, to the study of nature, to the anatomy of man, to the painting of life in an exact reproduction more original and powerful than anyone has so far dared to risk on the boards.

This is what I am waiting for. Some people shrug their shoulders, laugh, and reply that I shall wait forever. Their decisive argument is that I must not expect these things on the stage. The theatre is not the novel. The theatre has given us what it could give us. We must be content with the result. Now we are at the very center of the quarrel. I am trying to uproot the conditions of existence on the stage. If what I ask is impossible, then lies have a place on the boards: a play must have some romantic places, revolve around certain situations, and end at the proper time. My detractors take a "professional" view of the theatre: first, any analysis is boring, the audience demands facts, always facts; then there is the convention of the stage—an action must be played in three hours no matter what its length in time; then the characters are given a certain value which necessitates a fictional setting. I will not quote all the arguments. Now I come to the audience's intervention, which is considerable; the audience wishes this, the audience does not want that; it prefers four sympathetic puppets to one real character drawn from life. In a word, the stage is the domain of conventionality; everything is conventional from the decorations to the footlights which illuminate the actors who are led by a string. Truth can be shown only in small unnoticed doses. Some people even go so far as to swear that the theatre will die the day that it ceases to be an entertaining lie, destined to console the spectators in the evening for the sad realities of the day.

I am acquainted with all this reasoning, and I shall try to respond to it presently, when I reach my conclusion. Each genre of literature has its own conditions of existence. A novel, read alone in the comfort of one's own room, is not a play which is acted before two thousand spectators. The novelist has time and space before him. All kinds of liberties are permitted him; he can use one hundred pages, if he wishes, to analyze at his leisure a certain character; he can describe his surroundings as much as he pleases; he can cut his story short, can retrace his steps, changing scenes twenty times—in a word, he is absolute master of his medium. The dramatist, on the contrary, is enclosed in a rigid frame; he must obey all kinds of necessities. He moves only in the milieu of obstacles. Finally, there is the question of the isolated reader and the audience as a group; the solitary reader tolerates everything, goes where he is led, even when he is annoyed, whereas the audience as a whole is filled with prudishness, fright, and sensibilities which the author must recognize and unfortunately deal with. Since all this is true, it is precisely for this reason that the stage is the last citadel of conventionality as I stated earlier. If the naturalistic movement had not encountered in the theatre such difficult ground, covered with obstacles, naturalism would have taken root on the stage with the intensity and success it has had in the novel. The theatre, under its conditions of existence, must be the last, most labored and disputed conquest of the spirit of truth. . . .

Let us admit for a moment that the critics are right when they assert that naturalism is impossible in the theatre. Here is what these critics believe. Conventionality is a hard and fast rule on the stage; the lie will always have its place there. We are condemned to a continuance of Sardou's juggling, to the theories and witticisms of Dumas *fils,* and to the nice characters of Émile Augier. We will not create anything greater than the genius of these authors; we must accept them as the glory of our time on the stage. They are what they are because our theatre wishes them to be such. If they have not gone further in the drama, if they have not obeyed more perfectly the important wave of truth which is carrying us forward, it is the theatre which forbids them to be influenced by the truth. So in the theatre there is a barrier which blocks the road even to the strongest. Very well, then! But it is the theatre which you condemn; it is to the stage that you have given the mortal blow. You crush the theatre under the novel, you assign it an inferior place, you make it contemptible and useless in the eyes of generations to come. What do you wish us to do with the stage, we who are followers of the truth, anatomists, analysts, explorers of life, compilers of human data, if you prove to us that in the theatre we cannot use our methods or tools? Really! The theatre lives only on conventionalities; it must lie; it refuses to accept our experimental literature! Oh, well, then, the century will put the theatre aside, abandon it to the hands of the public entertainers, and will perform its great and superb work elsewhere. You pronounce the verdict, and you kill the stage. It is very evident that the naturalistic evolution will extend itself more and more because it is the very intelligence of the century. While the novelists are digging always further toward the truth, producing newer and more exact human documents, the theatre will flounder more every day in the center of its romantic fictions, worn-out plots, and skillfulness of construction. The situation will become more annoying because the public will certainly acquire a taste for reality in reading novels. The naturalistic movement is making itself forcibly felt. There will come a time when the public will shrug its shoulders and demand an innovation in the theatre. Either the stage will be naturalistic, or it will not exist at all; such is the formal conclusion.

I have the strongest faith in the future of our theatre. I no longer admit that the critics are right in saying that naturalism is impossible on the stage, and I am going to explain under what conditions the movement will, without any doubt, be brought about.

No, it is not true that the stage must remain stationary; it is not true that its actual conventionalities are the fundamental conditions of its existence. Everything goes on, I repeat; everything goes forward. The authors of today will be overruled; they cannot have the presumption to decide dramatic literature forever. What these authors have stammered about the opposition will clearly affirm; but the stage will not be shaken up because of the disagreement; it will enter, on the contrary, into a wider and straighter path. People have always resisted the march forward; they have denied to the newcomers the power and the right to accomplish what has not been performed by their elders. But the older generation will remain angry and blind in vain. The social and literary evolutions have an irresistible force; they can cross with one leap enormous obstacles which were said to be impassable. The theatre has been in vain what it is today; it will be tomorrow what it should be. And when the event takes place, everybody will think it perfectly natural.

Here I enter into mere probabilities, and I am no longer pretending to have the same scientific exactitude. As long as I have reasoned on facts, I have proved the truth of my position. Now I am content to foretell the future. The evolution will take place; that is certain. But will it pass to the left? Will it pass to the right? I do not really know. One can reason about it, nothing more.

Moreover, it is certain that the conditions existing on the stage will always be different. The novel, thanks to its free form, will remain perhaps the perfect tool of the century, while the stage will follow it and complete its action. The marvelous powers of the theatre must not be forgotten nor must its immediate effect upon the audience. No better instrument for propaganda exists. If the novel, then, is read by the fireside, in several instances, with a patience tolerating the longest details, the naturalistic drama should proclaim above all that it has no relation to this isolated

reader, but to a crowd who demand clearness and conciseness. I do not see that the naturalistic formula is antagonis-
tic to this conciseness and clearness. The novel analyzes
at length with a minuteness of detail which overlooks
nothing; the stage can analyze as briefly as it wishes by
actions and words. In Balzac's work a word or a cry is often
sufficient to describe the entire character. This cry belongs
essentially to the theatre. As to the acts, they are consistent with analysis in action, the most striking form of
action one can make. When we have gotten rid of the
child's play of a plot, the infantile game of tying up complicated threads in order to have the pleasure of untying
them again; when a play shall be only a real and logical
story, we shall have perfect analysis; we shall analyze forcibly the double influence of characters over facts, of facts
over characters. This idea is what has led me to say so
often that the naturalistic formula carries us back to the
source itself of our national stage with its classical formula.
In Corneille's tragedies and Molière's comedies, we find
this continuous analysis of character which I find necessary; plot takes a secondary place, and the work is a long
dissertation in dialogue on man. Only instead of an abstract man, I would substitute a natural man, put him in
his proper surroundings, and analyze all the physical and
social causes which make him what he is. To me, in a
word, the classical formula is a good one, on condition
that the scientific method is employed in the study of society itself, in the same way that the science of chemistry
is the study of compounds and their properties.

As to the long descriptions used in the novel, they cannot be used on the stage; that is evident. The naturalistic
novelists describe at length, not for the pleasure of
describing as they have been reproached for doing, but
because description is part of their formula to put down
full details about the character, and to make him complete by means of his environment. Such a novelist no
longer looks on man as an intellectual abstraction as he
was looked upon in the seventeenth century; he is a thinking animal, who forms part of nature, and who is subject to
the multiple influences of the soil in which he grows and
where he lives. That is why a climate, a country, a horizon,
are often decisively important. The novelist no longer separates his character from the air he breathes; he does not
describe him because of any rhetorical need, as the

didactic poets did, as Delille does, for example; he simply makes a note of the material conditions in which he finds his characters at every hour, and in which the facts are produced, in order to be absolutely thorough, and so that his inquiry may belong to the world's comprehensive view and reproduce reality in its entirety. Descriptions need not be transplanted to the stage; they are found there naturally. Is not the stage set a continual description more exact and startling than the descriptions in a novel? A set is only painted cardboard, some people say; indeed, but in a novel it is still less than painted cardboard—it is blackened paper despite which the illusion is created. After the scenery, set off so strikingly, and so surprisingly true, that we have recently seen in our theatres, no one can any longer deny the possibility of producing the reality of environment on the stage. It is up to dramatic authors now to utilize this reality; they will furnish the characters and the facts; the set designers, under the author's direction, will furnish the descriptions, as exact as shall be necessary. It is up to the dramatic author to make use of environments as novelists do, since the novelists know how to introduce and make such environments real.

I will add that, since the theatre is a material reproduction of life, external surroundings have always been a necessity there. In the seventeenth century, however, nature was not considered important, and, as man was looked upon only as a purely intellectual being, the scenery was vague—a peristyle of a temple, any kind of a room or public place would do. Today the naturalistic movement has brought about a more and more perfect exactness in stage scenery. Such fidelity was produced inevitably, little by little. I even find in this exactness proof of the unheralded task that naturalism has accomplished in the theatre since the beginning of the century. I cannot study thoroughly this question of scenery and accessories; I must content myself by stating that description is not only possible on the stage, but it is, moreover, a necessity which is imposed on the theatre as an essential condition of its existence.

I do not have to talk about the change of place. The unity of place has not been observed for a long time. The playwrights do not hesitate to depict an entire existence, to take the audience to both ends of the earth. Here con-

ventionality remains mistress as she is also in the novel. The
same idea applies to the question of time—but one must
cheat a little here. A plot which calls for fifteen days, for
example, must be played in the three hours which we set
apart for reading a novel or seeing it played at the
theatre. We are not the creative force which governs the
world; we are only second-rate creators who analyze, sum-
marize by trial and error, who are happy and acclaimed as
geniuses when we can disengage one ray of the truth.

I come now to the language. My detractors say that
there is a special style for the stage. They want it to be a
style completely different from that of daily conversation,
more sonorous, more sensitive, written in a higher key,
cut in facets, no doubt to make the theatre's chandeliers
sparkle. In our time, for example, Dumas *fils* has the
reputation of being a great playwright. His witticisms are
celebrated. They are shot off like skyrockets, falling in
showers to the audience's applause. Besides, all his characters speak the same language, the language of witty
Paris, spinning with paradoxes, always aiming for a good
hit, sharp and hard. I do not deny the sparkle of this
language—but it is a superficial sparkle which contains no
truth. Nothing is more fatiguing than these continual
mocking sentences. I would prefer greater flexibility and
naturalness. These sentences are at once too well and not
well enough written. The true stylists of our age are the
novelists—you must look to Gustave Flaubert and to the
Goncourts to find impeccable, living, and original style.
When you compare Dumas' style to that of these great
prose authors you find it does not stand up in correctness,
color, or emotion. What I want to hear in the theatre is
spoken language. If we are not able to reproduce on
the stage a conversation with its repetitions, its length,
and its useful words, the emotion and tone of the conversation could be kept; the individual turn of mind of
each speaker, the reality, in a word, reproduced to the
necessary extent. The Goncourts have made a curious
attempt at this style in *Henriette Maréchal,* that play
which no one wanted to listen to and which no one knows
anything about. The Greek actors spoke through a brass
tube; during the time of Louis XIV the comedians sang
their roles in a singsong tone to give them more pomp;
today we are content to say there is a language of the
theatre which is more sonorous and explosive. You can see

from these examples what progress we have made. One day the public will perceive that the best style in the theatre is that which best sets forth the spoken conversation, which puts the exact word in its proper place, giving it its just value. The naturalistic novelists have already written excellent models of dialogue, reduced to strictly useful words. The question of sentimental characters now remains. I do not disguise the fact that such a question is of capital importance. The public remains cold when its passion for an ideal character of loyalty and honor is not satisfied. A play which presents the audience with living characters taken from real life looks black and austere to it, when the play does not completely exasperate the public. It is on this point especially that the battle of naturalism is fought. We must learn to be patient. At the present time a secret change is taking place in the public's feeling; people are coming little by little, encouraged by the spirit of the century, to agree to a bold interpretation of real life and are even beginning to acquire a taste for it. When audiences can no longer stand certain lies, we shall have very nearly gained our point. Already the novelists' work is preparing the ground for our audiences. A time will come when a master playwright can reveal his ideas on the stage, finding there a public enthusiastically in favor of the truth. It will be a question of tact and strength. Such audiences will see then that the greatest and most useful lessons will be taught by depicting life as it is, and not by repeated generalities nor by speeches of bravado which are spoken merely to please our ears.

The two formulas are before us: the naturalistic formula which makes the stage a study and picture of real life; and the conventional formula which makes the stage an amusement for the mind, an intellectual guessing game, an art of adjustment and symmetry regulated after a certain code. In fact, everything depends on the idea one has of literature and of the drama in particular. If we admit that literature is an inquiry about things and human beings made by original minds, we are naturalists. If we pretend that literature is a framework superimposed upon the truth, that a writer must make use of observation merely in order to exhibit his power of invention and arrangement, we are idealists and proclaim the necessity of conventionality. . . .

And I add that we shall have life on the stage as we already have it in the novel. This would-be logic of actual plays, this equality and symmetry obtained by processes of reasoning, which come from ancient metaphysics, will collapse before the natural logic of facts and human beings such as reality gives us. In place of a theatre of fabrication, we shall have a stage of observation. How will the evolution be brought about? Tomorrow will give us the answer. I have tried to forecast the future, but leave to genius its realization. I have already stated my conclusion: our stage will be naturalistic, or it will cease to be.

Now that I have attempted to put my ideas together, may I hope people will no longer put words into my mouth which I have never spoken? Will they continue to see, in my critical judgment, I do not know what ludicrous inflations of vanity or repulsive retaliations? I am only the most sincere soldier of truth. If I am mistaken, my opinions are here in print; and fifty years from now I shall be judged, in my turn; I may be accused of injustice, blindness, and useless violence. I accept the verdict of the future.

Translated by Samuel Draper

AUGUST STRINDBERG
(1849-1912)

On Modern Drama and Modern Theatre[1] (1889)

... THERE ARE some who wish to date the new drama from the Goncourt brothers' *Henriette Maréchal*, performed at the Théâtre Français as early as 1865 and booed. But the reasons for this dating are not well founded, since the Goncourts represent a Christian physiological movement of older times and in the structure of their play simply used a few bold devices which every realistic movement before them has known how to utilize.

Rather the naturalistic drama will probably continue to regard *Thérèse Raquin* from 1873 as its first milestone. ... When Zola approaches the theatre to make a serious attempt to apply new methods, he is attracted immediately by a great and powerful motif, in this case a murder of one spouse in order that the other may gain the freedom to make another choice. But he does not proceed like Dumas or Augier, excusing the murder partly because of the prevailing legal system, which did not permit divorce; he neither excuses nor accuses, for he has canceled these concepts, but limits himself to a description of the development, indicating the motive of the act and showing its consequences. And in the pangs of conscience of the

[1] August Strindberg, "Om modernt drama och modern teater," *Samlade Skrifter* (Stockholm: Albert Bonniers Forlag, 1913), XVII, 281–303. In the incisive and thoroughly informative essay written in March, 1889, from which this selection is excerpted, Strindberg traces briefly the historical development of the French drama from the classical plays of Corneille, Racine, and Molière to the naturalistic innovations of André Antoine at the Théâtre Libre in Paris. During the course of the essay, Strindberg not only analyzes and evaluates the different schools of thought and movements in the French drama, but gives at the same time an illuminating account of the development of his own dramatic principles during the 1880's. After reading the essay, the reader has a clear picture of the nature of Strindberg's dramatic preferences by the year 1889, which he embodied in his own creative work of the late 1880's, beginning with *The Father* in 1887 and ending with his last *quart d'heure* play *Samum* in the spring of 1889 (Translator's note). Translation © 1960 by Borge Gedso Madsen.

criminals he sees merely an expression of disrupted social harmony, the results of habit and inherited ideas.

Thérèse Raquin is a new departure, but since it is adapted from a novel it is still not perfect in form. The author has had the feeling, however, that through greater unity of place his audience would receive a more complete illusion, by which the action would impress its main feature more forcefully on the spectators. At every curtain rise, the spectator had to be haunted by the memories of the preceding act and thus through the impact of the recurring milieu be captivated by the action. But because of the difficulty in having a before and after the crime sequence, Zola commits the error of letting a year elapse between the first and second acts. Presumably he did not dare offend against the prevailing law about a year's widowhood, otherwise a day between the acts would have been enough, and the play would have made a more unified impression. I therefore once suggested to a director of a theatre, whom I wanted to persuade to produce *Thérèse Raquin*, that he remove the first act. This can be done without any harm to the play, and recently I have seen a deceased French Zolaist make the same suggestion in a work on naturalism.[2]

With *Renée*, Zola seems to have returned to the form of the traditional Parisian comedy, with greater leaps in time and space than are compatible with the difficulty which a modern skeptical mind feels in allowing itself to be tricked into a belief in the conventions of the theatre. At the same time psychology is neglected in this play; the portrayal of character is superficial, and the whole thing is sketchy and melodramatic, which may be the usual result of adapting novels to the stage.

With *Thérèse Raquin* the great style, the deep probing of the human soul had attracted attention for a while, but no successors seem to venture forth. Still, the attempt has been made, since 1882, of regarding Henry Becque's *Les Corbeaux* as an epoch-making work. To me this seems to be a misunderstanding. If art is to be, as it has been said, a piece of nature seen through a temperament, then there really is a piece of nature in Becque's *Crows,* but the temperament is lacking.

A factory owner dies in the first act after, among many other incidents, his son has appeared in the first scene comically got up in his father's dressing gown. This com-

[2] Louis Desprez, *L'Évolution naturaliste* (Strindberg's note).

pletely superfluous little prank, the significance of which I fail to grasp, was probably included by the dramatist because it happened in real life from which this boring and rather unimportant episode has been taken. After the death of the factory owner, his partner, lawyers, paid and unpaid creditors appear on the scene and seize the inheritance, so that the family becomes insolvent. That is all!

Here we have the ordinary case which is so much in demand these days, the *rule,* the human norm, which is so banal, so insignificant, so dull that after four hours of suffering you ask yourself the old question: how does this concern me? This is the objective which is so beloved by those devoid of temperament, the soulless as they shall be called!

This is photography which includes everything, even the grain of dust on the lens of the camera. This is realism, a working method elevated to art, or the little art which does not see the forest for the trees. This is the misunderstood naturalism which holds that art merely consists of drawing a piece of nature in a natural way; it is not the great naturalism which seeks out the points where the great battles are fought, which loves to see what you do not see every day, which delights in the struggle between natural forces, whether these forces are called love and hate, rebellious or social instincts, which finds the beautiful or ugly unimportant if only it is great. It is this grandiose art which we found in *Germinal* and *La Terre,* and which we expected to see reappear in the theatre, but which did not come with Becque's *Corbeaux* or Zola's *Renée,* but which gradually was to come into existence through the opening of a new stage, which, under the name of the Théâtre Libre, is active in the heart of Paris.

. . . There are few theatres at which dramatic works are produced in all their natural freshness, their innate directness, in their original form, in other words. First of all they have to pass through the sieve of censorships and then be subjected to the collaboration of a systematic, experienced, and, what is worse, perhaps ignorant director. At the Théâtre Libre they appear in all their pleasing naïveté and completeness, without embellishments and puerile abbreviations. If the success is but small, the result is a severe but useful lesson to the writer; if on the other hand it is great, the author gets all the credit. Double gain!

And both the credit and the lesson are so much more

valuable because they do not owe anything to a charming staging of the play.

Here one does not find those superb settings which dazzle the eye and make the spectators overlook the emptiness of the action; none of those widely famous virtuosities which, like a scarlet cloak, hide the poverty of the form.

Here the staging of plays is very simple, and the performers consist of a handful of young devotees who combine all the naïveté of inexperience with the conviction and enthusiasm of youth.

Shakespeare was not interpreted better than this when he wrote his masterpieces.

Rapidly a repertoire[3] had arisen so that about twenty plays were performed in a year, *and naturalism which had been declared impossible on the stage by critics and other timid persons, now asserted itself triumphantly there.* Already one sees indications of a search for a form which seems to take the new drama in a direction somewhat different from the first attempts in *Thérèse Raquin* and which breaks away completely from Zola's adaptations of both *L'Assommoir* and *Germinal* with their crowd effects and elaborate theatrical apparatus.

Hardly a full-length play is seen, and Zola himself makes his debut with a one-act play; and when three-act plays were performed, a strong predilection for the unities of time and place was noticeable. Besides, intrigue seems to have been abandoned and the main interest focused on the psychological description of character.

In old Greek the word *drama* seems to have meant event, not action or what we call conscious intrigue. For life does not move as regularly as a constructed drama, and conscious spinners of intrigue very seldom get a chance to carry out their plans in detail. Thus we no longer believe in these cunning plotters who, unhindered, are permitted to control people's destinies, so that the villain in his conscious falseness merely arouses our ridicule as not being true to life.

In the new naturalistic drama a striving for the signifi-

---

[3] The complete repertoire of the Théâtre Libre will be found in Samuel M. Waxman, *Antoine and the Théâtre Libre* (Cambridge: Harvard University Press, 1926), Appendix A, pp. 221–29.

cant motif was felt at once. Therefore, the action was usually centered around life's two poles, life and death, the act of birth and the act of death, the fight for the spouse, for the means of subsistence, for honor, all these struggles—with their battlefields, cries of woe, wounded and dead—during which one heard the new philosophy of life conceived as a struggle, blow its fertile winds from the south.

These were tragedies such as had not been seen before. The young authors of a generation whose school had so far been a school of suffering—the most terrible, perhaps, which exists: severe intellectual oppression, even in such cruel forms as persecution with imprisonment and starvation—these young authors themselves seemed reluctant to impose their suffering on others more than was absolutely necessary. Therefore, they made the suffering as brief as possible, let the pain pour forth in one act, sometimes in a single scene. Such a little masterpiece was, for example, *Entre Frères* by Guiches and Lavedan. The play is so brief that it is performed in fifteen minutes, and the genre immediately was called *quart d'heure*.

The action, if it can be called action, is as follows: In a bed lies an old woman dying, and beside her stand her three sons. The dying person makes a sign that she wants to speak, and then she reveals the secret of her life: one of the sons was conceived in adultery. She falls back unconscious, apparently dead, before she has had time to tell which of the sons is the illegitimate one.

The sons deliberate and on certain grounds decide that the youngest one is legitimate. The marquis, the head of the family, suggests that they keep the secret, but that the illegitimate heir leave.

At that moment the mother comes to and is able to utter only these words: "It is the marquis!" The end!

This is the drama reduced to one scene, and why not? One who has had the job of reading plays which are submitted to a theatrical director soon observes that every play seems to have been written for the sake of a single scene, and that all the author's creative joy centered around this scene which sustained him during the terrible pains which exposition, presentation, entanglement, disentanglement, *peripeteia,* and catastrophe caused him.

For the satisfaction of having written a full-length play, he bores his audience by arousing its curiosity about matters it already knows, harasses the director by making him maintain a large personnel, makes life miserable for those unfortunate actors who play the secondary parts, as well as the critics, the confidants, the *raisonneurs*, without whom no intrigue or full-length play can materialize, and to whom he must go to the trouble of giving a character.

Therefore carefully constructed five-act plays are very rare; and one has to put up with a lot of superfluous nonsense to get to the gist of the matter. Since I have recently read about twenty-five plays, among them one of four hundred pages with seventeen characters, I have been confirmed in certain suspicions about the reason for the lack of good drama. Every beginner seems to me to be able to write one good act; in that one he is true to life, every word is straightforward, and the action is honest. As soon as he embarks on the writing of long plays, everything becomes labored, contrived, affected, and false. The two-act plays form a genre by themselves, but not a very happy one. It is the head and the tail, with the body missing; it is before and after the catastrophe, usually with a year between. Ordinarily the second act contains the moral lesson: this is how it goes if you do this and that in the first act. Most beautiful in construction are the three-act plays observing the unities of time and place, when the subject is a big one. For example, Ibsen's *Ghosts* should be compared with *Rosmersholm* which was found to be far too long. The taste of the period, this headlong, hectic period, seems to move toward the brief and expressive. Tolstoy's painful *Power of Darkness* at the Théâtre Libre proved incapable of keeping interest alive and even had to fall back on Franco-Russian politics for effect.

A scene, a *quart d'heure*, seems to be the type of play preferred by modern theatregoers, and it has an old history. For it can name as its origin (yes, why not?) the Greek tragedy which contains a concentrated event in a single act, if we regard the trilogy as three separate plays. But if we do not want to go way back to Paradise, we have in the eighteenth century a gentleman called Carmontelle, who was the first to cultivate on a large scale the genre he named *Proverbes Dramatiques*, of which he published ten volumes and is supposed to have left a hundred more in manuscript. The genre was later developed by Leclerq, attained its highest perfection in Musset's and Feuillet's well-known masterpieces—and more recently in Henry Becque's *La Navette* to form the transition to the fully executed one-act play,[4] which may become the formula for the drama to come.

In the proverb one got the gist of the matter, the whole dénouement, the battle of the souls, sometimes approaching tragedy in Musset, without having to be bothered by the clanging of arms or processions of supernumeraries. By means of a table and two chairs one could present the most powerful conflicts life has to offer; and in this type of art all the discoveries of modern psychology could, for the first time, be applied in popularized form.

As is well known, in our day the proverb developed rapidly, was used and misused; it became easily available, and the result was a surfeit of it. The proverb proved, however, to be the seed of a prospective form—when the author and the public favored the same thing—but it declined, was buried and ridiculed, because no one dared use it for greater efforts, as Musset had done, although not always successfully.

By this I do not mean to say that *this is the only possible approach*. The Théâtre Libre did not start its activity by proclaiming any program; it has never developed an aesthetic, never wanted to form a school. Writers have therefore taken advantage of this freedom, and the theatre's poster has shown the most varied forms, new and old together, even as old as the tragic parade, the mystery, and the pantomime. And from the laws of modern aesthetics has also been eliminated the decree that it is not permissible to place an action in the historical past. All prohibitive laws have been canceled, and only the demands of taste and of the modern spirit are allowed to determine the artistic form.

Is this not possibly an emancipation of art, a renaissance, a liberation from a terrible aesthetics which was beginning to make people unhappy, which wanted to change the theatre into a political arena, into a Sunday school, a chapel? Perhaps!

May we too get such a theatre where one can shudder at the most horrible, laugh at the ridiculous, play with toys; where one can get to see everything and not be offended if one gets to see what has so far been hidden behind theological and aesthetic veils, even though the old laws

[4] *Den utförda enaktaren*. By this expression Strindberg probably means a one-act play slightly longer than the *quart d'heure* and with regular division into scenes (Translator's note).

of convention be broken; may we get a free theatre where one has freedom for everything, except the freedom to lack talent and be a hypocrite or a fool!

And if we should not get any such theatre, we shall probably manage to survive anyway!

Translated by Børge Gedsø Madsen

ANTON CHEKHOV
(1860-1904)

Advice to Playwrights[1]

TO A. P. CHEKHOV, APRIL 11, 1889

TRY TO be original in your play and as clever as possible; but don't be afraid to show yourself foolish; we must have freedom of thinking, and only he is an emancipated thinker who is not afraid to write foolish things. Don't round things out, don't polish—but be awkward and impudent. Brevity is the sister of talent. Remember, by the way, that declarations of love, the infidelity of husbands and wives; widows', orphans', and all other tears, have long since been written up. The subject ought to be new, but there need be no "fable." And the main thing is—father and mother must eat. Write. Flies purify the air, and plays —the morals.

TO A. P. CHEKHOV, MAY 8, 1889

Now about your play. You undertook to depict a man who has not a grief in the world, and then you took fright. The problem seems to me to be clear. Only he has no grief who is indifferent; and people who are indifferent and aloof are either philosophers or petty, egotistic natures. The latter should be treated negatively, the former—positively. Of course, those unmoved dullards who will suffer no pain even when you burn them with red-hot irons cannot be discussed at all. Even if by a man without grief you understand one who is not indifferent to the life about him, and who bravely and patiently bears the blows of fate, and looks hopefully to the future—there, too, the problem is comparatively simple and clear.

The large number of revisions need not trouble you,

[1] Anton Chekhov, *Letters on the Short Story, the Drama and other Literary Topics,* selected and edited by Louis S. Friedland (New York: Minton, Balch & Co., 1924), pp. 170–80.

for the more of a mosaic the work is, the better. The characters stand to gain by this. The play will be worthless if all the characters resemble you. In this respect your *Money-Box* is monotonous and arouses a feeling of boredom. What are Natasha, Kolya, Tosya for? Is there no life outside of you? And who is interested in knowing my life or yours, my thoughts and your thoughts? Give people people, and not yourself.

Avoid "choice" diction. The language should be simple and forceful. The lackeys should speak simply, without elegance. Retired captains in the reserve, with huge, red noses, newspaper reporters who drink, starving authors, consumptive women toilers, honest young people without a flaw in their make-up, ideal maidens, good-natured nurses —all these have been described again and again, and should be avoided as a pitfall. Still another suggestion: go to the theatre now and then and watch the stage. Compare—that is important. The first act may last as long as a whole hour, but the rest should not be more than twenty minutes each. The crux of the play is the third act, but it must not be so strong a climax as to kill the last act.

TO A. S. SOUVORIN, MAY 30, 1888

As to your play,[2] I try in vain to see why you speak so ill of it. Its defects do not spring from your not being sufficiently talented, or from your not having great enough powers of observation, but from the nature of your creative ability. You are more inclined to austere creation, which was developed in you by extensive reading of classic models, and by your love for these models. Imagine your *Tatyana* written in verse, and you will see that its defects will take on a different aspect. If it were written in verse, nobody would notice that all its characters speak one and the same language, nobody would reproach your characters for uttering nothing but philosophy, and for "feuilletonizing" in the classic form—all this would blend with the classic tone as smoke blends with the air—and one would not observe in your *Tatyana* the absence of the commonplace language and the everyday, petty actions that the modern drama must provide in plenty. . . . Give your characters Latin names, attire them in togas, and you will get the same thing—the defects of your play are

[2] *Tatyana Repina.*

irremediable because they are organic. Console yourself with the fact that they are the product of your actual qualities, and that if you gave these qualities to other playwrights, their plays would become more interesting and clever.

TO A. S. SOUVORIN, DECEMBER 19, 1888

The first act of your *Repina* is put together so strangely that I am altogether at a loss. In rehearsal this act seemed to me dreary and unskillfully done, but now I understand that one cannot make plays otherwise, and I comprehend the success of this act. After *Tatyana* I consider my own play[3] as so much sweetmeats, although I have not as yet made clear to myself whether your play is good or not. In its architectonics there is something that I do not quite grasp.

TO A. S. SOUVORIN, JANUARY 6, 1889

I like the "vaudeville." It begins in a very original way. Very hackneyed are: the cousin, the glove, the card falling out of the pocket, the eavesdropping. . . . In one-act things you must write *nonsense*,—there lies their strength. Manage it so that the wife wants seriously to run away,— she has become bored, and desires new experiences. She threatens seriously to cuckold her second husband. . . . The talk about the cuckolding is good. The eavesdropping is unnecessary; let the husband arrive just after the wife has finished writing her letter, and has gone out for a minute to her friends to ask forgiveness, then to return home for her baggage. The dialogue is suitable and pat.

TO A. S. SOUVORIN, JANUARY 23, 1900

The new play,[4] Acts I and II, I liked, and I find that it is even better than *Tatyana Repina*. The other is closer to the theatre, this to life. The third act was not definite, because there is no action; there is not even clarity of idea. It may be that to make it more certain and clearer, a fourth act will be required. In the third act the explanation between the husband and the wife is modeled after Sumbatov's *Chains*; and I would prefer that the wife remain be-

[3] *Ivanov.*
[4] *The Question.*

hind the curtain all the time, and that Varya, as happens in life in similar circumstances, should believe more in the father than in the mother.

I have few comments to make. A cultured nobleman entering the priesthood, that has become stale, and no longer arouses curiosity. Those who entered the priesthood just fell into the water; some, remaining ordinary abbots, waxed fat and have long since forgotten every idea; others gave up all and are living in peace. Nothing definite was expected of them, and they gave nothing; and on the stage a young man preparing for the priesthood will simply be received without sympathy by the public, and in his activities and chastity they will see something of the Skoptsi.[5] And, indeed, the actor will not play the part well. You would do better to take a young, learned, mysterious Jesuit dreaming of a united church; or someone else, but someone who will appear greater than a nobleman entering the priesthood.

Varya is well done. At first sight there is an excessive hysteria in the language. She must not use witticisms; but you make all of them fall into this habit; they keep playing on words, and that tires the attention a little; it is too flashy; the language of your charcters is like a white silk dress on which the sun is always shining in full force and which it hurts the eyes to look at. The words "vulgarity" and "vulgar" are hackneyed.

Natasha is very good. You make her a different person in the third act.

The families "Ratishchev" and "Muratov" are too theatrical, not simple. Give Ratishchev to a Little Russian family, for variety.

The father is without a weakness, without a distinct appearance; he does not drink, or smoke, or gamble, or fall ill. You must stitch onto him some attribute or other, so that the actor can have something to grasp.

The father knows of Varya's sin or does not know,—I think it makes no difference, and is of no importance. The sexual sphere, of course, plays an important part in this world, but not everything depends on it,—far from everything; and not everywhere, by far, does it have decisive significance.

When you send the fourth act I shall write more if I think of anything to say. I am glad that you have almost

[5] A fanatic, ascetic religious sect in Russia.

completed the play, and again repeat that you ought to
write both plays and novels, first because it is necessary,
and second, because for you it is healthful, as it is pleasant
to vary your life.

TO MAXIM GORKY, FEBRUARY 15, 1900

I am very sorry that apparently you have given up the
idea of coming to Yalta. The Art Theatre from Moscow
will be here in May. It will give five performances and then
remain for rehearsals. So you come, study the stage at
the rehearsals, and then in five to eight days write a play,
which I should welcome joyfully with my whole heart.

TO MAXIM GORKY, SEPTEMBER 8, 1900

I have just been reading in the papers that you are
writing a play. Write, write, write! It is necessary. Even
should the play fail, don't let that discourage you. A failure will be soon forgotten, but a success, however slight,
may be of vast service to the theatre.

TO MAXIM GORKY, SEPTEMBER 24, 1900

By all means, *golubchik,* finish the play. You feel that
it is not turning out as you should like, but don't trust
your feeling, as it may deceive you. One usually dislikes a
play while writing it, but afterward it grows on one. Let
others judge and make decisions.

TO MAXIM GORKY, OCTOBER 22, 1901

Five days have passed since I read your play *The Petty
Bourgeois.* I have not written to you till now because I
could not get hold of the fourth act; I have kept waiting
for it, and—I still have not got it. And so I have read
only three acts, but that I think is enough to judge of the
play. It is, as I expected, very good, written à la Gorky,
original, very interesting; and, to begin by talking of the
defects, I have noticed only one, a defect incorrigible as
red hair in a red-haired man—the conservatism of the
form. You make new and original people sing new songs to
an accompaniment that looks secondhand; you have four
acts, the characters deliver edifying discourses, there is a
feeling of alarm before long speeches, and so on, and so
on. But all that is not important, and it is all, so to speak,

drowned in the good points of the play. Perchikhin—how
live! His daughter is enchanting, Tatyana and Piotr also,
and their mother is a spendid old woman. The central figure of the play, Nil, is vigorously drawn and extremely interesting! In fact, the play takes hold of one from the first
act. Only, God preserve you from letting anyone act
Perchikhin except Artyom, while Alexeyev-Stanislavsky
must certainly play Nil. Those two figures will do just what's
needed; Piotr—Meyerhold. Only, Nil's part, a wonderful
part, must be made two or three times as long. You ought
to end the play with it, to make it the leading part. Only,
do not contrast him with Piotr and Tatyana, let him be
by himself and them by themselves, all wonderful, splendid
people independent of one another. When Nil tries to seem
superior to Piotr and Tatyana, and says of himself that he
is a fine fellow—the element so characteristic of our decent
workingman, the element of modesty, is lost. He boasts, he
argues, but you know one can see what sort of man he is
without that. Let him be merry, let him play pranks through
the whole four acts, let him eat a great deal after his
work—and that will be enough for him to conquer the audience with. Piotr, I repeat, is good. Most likely you don't
even suspect how good he is. Tatyana, too, is a finished
figure, only—(a) she ought really to be a schoolmistress,
ought to be teaching children, ought to come home from
school, ought to be taken up with her pupils and exercise
books, and—(b) it ought to be mentioned in the first or
second act that she has attempted to poison herself; then,
after that hint, the poisoning in the third act will not seem
so startling and will be more in place. Teterev talks too
much: such characters ought to be shown bit by bit among
others, for in any case such people are everywhere merely
incidental—both in life and on the stage. Make Elena dine
with all the rest in the first act, let her sit and make jokes,
or else there is very little of her, and she is not clear.
Her avowal to Piotr is too abrupt; on the stage it would
come out in too high relief. Make her a passionate woman,
if not loving, at least apt to fall in love. . . .

TO MAXIM GORKY, JULY 29, 1902

I have read your play.[6] It is new and unmistakably fine.
The second act is very good; it is the best, the strongest,

6 *The Lower Depths.*

and when I was reading it, especially the end, I almost danced with joy. The tone is gloomy, oppressive; the audience, unaccustomed to such subjects, will walk out of the theatre, and you may well say good-by to your reputation as an optimist, in any case. My wife will play Vassilisa, the immoral and spiteful woman; Vishnevsky walks about the house and imagines himself the Tartar—he is convinced that it is the part for him. Luka, alas! you must not give to Artyom. He will repeat himself in that part and be exhausted; but he would do the policeman wonderfully; it is his part. The part of the actor, in which you have been very successful (it is a magnificent part), should be given to an experienced actor, Stanislavsky perhaps. Kachalov will play the baron.

You left out of the fourth act all the most interesting characters (except the actor), and you must mind, now, that there is no ill effect from it. The act may seem boring and unnecessary, especially if, with the exit of the strongest and most interesting actors, there are left only the mediocrities. The death of the actor is awful; it is as though you gave the spectator a sudden box on the ear apropos of nothing without preparing him in any way. How the baron got into the doss house and why he is a baron is also not quite clear.

TO V. NEMIROVICH-DANCHENKO, NOVEMBER 2, 1903

Apropos of the popular theatres and popular literature—all that is foolishness, sugar candy for the people. You must not lower Gogol to the people, but raise the people to the level of Gogol.

MAURICE MAETERLINCK
(1862-1949)

The Tragic in Daily Life[1] (1896)

. . . When I go to the theatre, I feel as though I were
spending a few hours with my ancestors, who conceived
life as something that was primitive, arid, and brutal; but
this conception of theirs scarcely even lingers in my memory, and surely it is not one that I can share. I am shown
a deceived husband killing his wife, a woman poisoning her
lover, a son avenging his father, a father slaughtering his
children, children putting their father to death, murdered
kings, ravished virgins, imprisoned citizens—in a word, all
the sublimity of tradition, but alas, how superficial and
material! Blood, surface tears, and death! What can I learn
from creatures who have but one fixed idea, and who have
no time to live, for there is a rival, or a mistress, whom
it behooves them to put to death?

I had hoped to be shown some act of life, traced back
to its sources and to its mystery by connecting links, that
my daily occupations afford me neither power nor occasion
to study. I had gone there hoping that the beauty, the
grandeur, and the earnestness of my humble day-by-day
existence would, for one instant, be revealed to me, that I
would be shown the I know not what presence, power, or
God that is ever with me in my room. I was yearning for
one of the strange moments of a higher life that flit unper-
ceived through my dreariest hours; whereas, almost invariably, all that I beheld was but a man who would tell me,
at wearisome length, why he was jealous, why he poisoned,
or why he killed.

I admire Othello, but he does not appear to me to live
the august daily life of a Hamlet, who has the time to live,
inasmuch as he does not act. Othello is admirably jealous.

[1] Maurice Maeterlinck, "The Tragical in Daily Life," *The
Treasure of the Humble,* translated by Alfred Sutro (New
York: Dodd, Mead and Co., 1916), pp. 103–19.

But is it not perhaps an ancient error to imagine that it is at the moments when this passion, or others of equal violence, possesses us, that we live our truest lives? I have grown to believe that an old man, seated in his armchair, waiting patiently, with his lamp beside him; giving unconscious ear to all the eternal laws that reign about his house, interpreting, without comprehending, the silence of doors and windows and the quivering voice of the light, submitting with bent head to the presence of his soul and his destiny—an old man, who conceives not that all the powers of this world, like so many heedful servants, are mingling and keeping vigil in his room, who suspects not that the very sun itself is supporting in space the little table against which he leans, or that every star in heaven and every fiber of the soul are directly concerned in the movement of an eyelid that closes, or a thought that springs to birth—I have grown to believe that he, motionless as he is, does yet live in reality a deeper, more human, and more universal life than the lover who strangles his mistress, the captain who conquers in battle, or "the husband who avenges his honor."

I shall be told, perhaps, that a motionless life would be invisible, that therefore animation must be conferred upon it, and movement, and that such varied movement as would be acceptable is to be found only in the few passions of which use has hitherto been made. I do not know whether it be true that a static theatre is impossible. Indeed, to me it seems to exist already. Most of the tragedies of Aeschylus are tragedies without movement. In both the *Prometheus* and the *Suppliants,* events are lacking; and the entire tragedy of the *Choephori*—surely the most terrible drama of antiquity—does but cling, nightmarelike, around the tomb of Agamemnon, till murder darts forth, as a lightning flash, from the accumulation of prayers, ever falling back upon themselves. Consider, from this point of view, a few more of the finest tragedies of the ancients: *The Eumenides, Antigone, Electra, Oedipus at Colonus.* "They have admired," said Racine in his preface to *Berenice*, "they have admired the *Ajax* of Sophocles, wherein there is nothing but Ajax killing himself with regret for the fury into which he fell after the arms of Achilles were denied him. They have admired *Philoctetes,* whose entire subject is but the coming of Ulysses with intent to seize the arrows of Hercules. Even the *Oedipus,* though full of recognitions, contains less subject matter than the simplest tragedy of our days."

What have we here but life that is almost motionless? In most cases, indeed, you will find that psychological action—infinitely loftier in itself than mere material action, and truly, one might think, well-nigh indispensable—that psychological action even has been suppressed, or at least vastly diminished, in a truly marvelous fashion, with the result that the interest centers solely and entirely in the individual, face to face with the universe. Here we are no longer with the barbarians, nor is man now fretting himself in the midst of elementary passions, as though, forsooth, these were the only things worthy of note: he is at rest, and we have time to observe him. It is no longer a violent, exceptional moment of life that passes before our eyes —it is life itself. Thousands and thousands of laws there are, mightier and more venerable than those of passion; but these laws are silent, and discreet, and slow-moving; and hence it is only in the twilight that they can be seen and heard, in the meditation that comes to us at the tranquil moments of life.

When Ulysses and Neoptolemus come to Philoctetes and demand of him the arms of Hercules, their action is in itself as simple and ordinary as that of a man of our day who goes into a house to visit an invalid, of a traveler who knocks at the door of an inn, or of a mother who, by the fireside, awaits the return of her child. Sophocles indicates the character of his heroes by means of the lightest and quickest of touches. But it may safely be said that the chief interest of the tragedy does not lie in the struggle we witness between cunning and loyalty, between love of country, rancor, and headstrong pride. There is more beyond: for it is man's loftier existence that is laid bare to us. The poet adds to ordinary life something, I know not what, which is the poet's secret: and there comes to us a sudden revelation of life in its stupendous grandeur, in its submissiveness to the unknown powers, in its endless affinities, in its awe-inspiring mystery. Let but the chemist pour a few mysterious drops into a vessel that seems to contain the purest water, and at once masses of crystals will rise to the surface, thus revealing to us all that lay in abeyance there where nothing was visible before to our incomplete eyes. And even thus is it in *Philoctetes*; the primitive psychology of the three leading characters would seem to be merely the sides of the vessel containing the clear water; and this itself is our ordinary life, into which the poet is about to let fall the revelation-bearing drops of his genius. ...

Indeed, it is not in the actions but in the words that are found the beauty and greatness of tragedies that are truly beautiful and great; and this not solely in the words that accompany and explain the action, for there must perforce be another dialogue besides the one which is superficially necessary. And indeed the only words that count in the play are those that at first seemed useless, for it is therein that the essence lies. Side by side with the necessary dialogue will you almost always find another dialogue that seems superfluous; but examine it carefully, and it will be borne home to you that this is the only one that the soul can listen to profoundly, for here alone is it the soul that is being addressed. You will see, too, that it is the quality and the scope of this unnecessary dialogue that determine the quality and the immeasurable range of the work. Certain it is that, in the ordinary drama, the indispensable dialogue by no means corresponds to reality; and it is just those words that are spoken by the side of the rigid, apparent truth, that constitute the mysterious beauty of the most beautiful tragedies, inasmuch as these are words that conform to a deeper truth, and one that lies incomparably nearer to the invisible soul by which the poem is upheld. One may even affirm that a poem draws the nearer to beauty and loftier truth in the measure that it eliminates words that merely explain the action, and substitutes for them others that reveal, not the so-called "soul-state," but I know not what intangible and unceasing striving of the soul toward its own beauty and truth. And so much the nearer, also, does it draw to the true life. To every man does it happen, in his workaday existence, that some situation of deep seriousness has to be unraveled by means of words. Reflect for an instant. At moments such as those—nay, at the most commonplace of times—is it the thing you say or the reply you receive that has the most value? Are not other forces, other words one cannot hear, brought into being, and do not these determine the event? What I say often counts for so little; but my presence, the attitude of my soul, my future and my past, that which will take birth in me and that which is dead, a secret thought, the stars that

approve, my destiny, the thousands of mysteries which
surround me and float about yourself—all this it is that
speaks to you at that tragic moment, all this it is that brings
to me your answer. There is all this beneath every one of
my words, and each one of yours; it is this, above all,
that we see, it is this above all, that we hear, ourselves
notwithstanding. If you have come, you, the "outraged
husband," the "deceived lover," the "forsaken wife," in-
tending to kill me, your arm will not be stayed by my
most moving entreaty; but it may be that there will come
toward you, at that moment, one of these unexpected
forces; and my soul, knowing of their vigil near to me, may
whisper a secret word whereby, haply, you shall be dis-
armed. These are the spheres wherein adventures come to
issue, this is the dialogue whose echo should be heard. And
it is this echo that one does hear—extremely attenuated and
variable, it is true—in some of the great works mentioned
above. But might we not try to draw nearer to the spheres
where it is "in reality" that everything comes to pass?

It would seem as though the endeavor were being made.
Some time ago, when dealing with *The Master Builder,*
which is the one of Ibsen's dramas wherein this dialogue of
the "second degree" attains the deepest tragedy, I endeavored, unskillfully enough, to fix its secrets. For indeed
they are kindred handmarks traced on the same wall
by the same sightless being, groping for the same light.
"What is it," I asked, "what is it that, in *The Master
Builder,* the poet has added to life, thereby making it
appear so strange, so profound, and so disquieting beneath its trivial surface?" The discovery is not easy, and
the old master hides from us more than one secret. It
would even seem as though what he has wished to say
were but little by the side of what he has been compelled
to say. He has freed certain powers of the soul that have
never yet been free, and it may well be that these have
held him in thrall. "Look you, Hilda," exclaims Solness,
"look you! There is sorcery in you, too, as there is in me.
It is this sorcery that imposes action on the powers of the
beyond. And we *have* to yield to it. Whether we want to or
not, we *must*."

There is sorcery in them, as in us all. Hilda and Solness
are, I believe, the first characters in drama who feel, for
an instant, that they are living in the atmosphere of the
soul; and the discovery of this essential life that exists in

them, beyond the life of every day, comes fraught with terror. Hilda and Solness are two souls to whom a flash has revealed their situation in the true life. Diverse ways there are by which knowledge of our fellows may come to us. Two or three men, perhaps, are seen by me almost daily. For a long time it is merely by their gestures that I distinguish them, by their habits, be these of mind or body, by the manner in which they feel, act, or think. But, in the course of every friendship of some duration, there comes to us a mysterious moment when we seem to perceive the exact relationship of our friend to the unknown that surrounds him, when we discover the attitude destiny has assumed toward him. And it is from this moment that he truly belongs to us. We have seen, once and for all, the treatment held in store for him by events. We know that however such a one may seclude himself in the recesses of his dwelling, in dread lest his slightest movement stir up that which lies in the great reservoirs of the future, his forethought will avail him nothing, and the innumerable events that destiny holds in reserve will discover him wherever he hides, and will knock one after another at his door. And even so do we know that this other will sally forth in vain in pursuit of adventure. He will ever return empty-handed. No sooner are our eyes thus opened than unerring knowledge would seem to spring to life, self-created, within our soul; and we know with absolute conviction that the event that seems to be impending over the head of a certain man will nevertheless most assuredly not reach him.

From this moment a special part of the soul reigns over the friendship of even the most unintelligent, the obscurest of men. Life has become, as it were, transposed. And when it happens that we meet one of the men who are thus known to us, though we do but speak of the snow that is falling or the women that pass by, something there is in each of us which nods to the other, which examines and asks its questions without our knowledge, which interests itself in contingencies and hints at events that it is impossible for us to understand. . . .

Thus do I conceive it to be with Hilda and Solness; it is thus surely that they regard each other. Their conversation resembles nothing that we have ever heard, inasmuch as the poet has endeavored to blend in one expression both the inner and the outer dialogue. A new, indescribable power dominates this somnambulistic drama. All that is

said therein at once hides and reveals the sources of an
unknown life. And if we are bewildered at times, let us not
forget that our soul often appears to our feeble eyes to be
but the maddest of forces, and that there are in man
many regions more fertile, more profound, and more interesting than those of his reason or his intelligence. . . .

WILLIAM BUTLER YEATS
(1865-1939)

Language, Character, and Construction[1] (1904)

WHAT ATTRACTS me to drama is that it is, in the most
obvious way, what all the arts are upon a last analysis. A
farce and a tragedy are alike in this, that they are a
moment of intense life. An action is taken out of all other
actions; it is reduced to its simplest form, or at any rate
to as simple a form as it can be brought to without our
losing the sense of its place in the world. The characters
that are involved in it are freed from everything that is
not a part of that action; and whether it is, as in the less
important kinds of drama, a mere bodily activity, a hair-
breadth escape or the like, or as it is in the more important
kinds, an activity of the souls of the characters, it is an
energy, an eddy of life purified from everything but itself.
The dramatist must picture life in action, with an un-
preoccupied mind, as the musician pictures her in sound
and the sculptor in form.

Our plays[2] must be literature or written in the spirit of
literature. The modern theatre has died away to what it is
because the writers have thought of their audiences instead of their subject. An old writer saw his hero, if it was
a play of character, or some dominant passion, if it was
a play of passion, like *Phèdre* or *Andromaque*, moving
before him, living with a life he did not endeavor to control. The persons acted upon one another as they were

[1] W. B. Yeats, *Plays and Controversies* (London: Macmillan & Co., Ltd. 1923), pp. 91–93, 103, 117–24. Copyright
1924 by The Macmillan Co., 1952 by Bertha Georgie Yeats. Reprinted by permission of The Macmillan Co.
[2] In a letter offering the Abbey Theatre to the Irish National
Theatre Company, Miss Horniman asked Yeats to state his
plans for the theatre. "The Play, the Player and the Scene,"
from which this excerpt on the play is drawn, constitutes Yeats's
program for the theatre.

bound by their natures to act, and the play was dramatic,
not because he had sought out dramatic situations for
their own sake, but because will broke itself upon will
and passion upon passion. Then the imagination began to
cool, the writer began to be less alive, to seek external aids,
remembered situations, tricks of the theatre, that had
proved themselves again and again. His persons no longer
will have a particular character, but he knows that he can
rely upon the incidents, and he feels himself fortunate
when there is nothing in his play that has not succeeded
a thousand times before the curtain has risen. Perhaps he
has even read a certain guidebook to the stage published
in France, and called *The Thirty-six Situations of Drama.*
The costumes will be magnificent, the actresses will be
beautiful, the Castle in Spain will be painted by an artist
upon the spot. We will come from his play excited if we are
foolish, or can condescend to the folly of others, but
knowing nothing new about ourselves, and seeing life with
no new eyes and hearing it with no new ears. The whole
movement of theatrical reform in our day has been a
struggle to get rid of this kind of play, and the sincere
play, the logical play, that we would have in its place, will
always seem, when we hear it for the first time, undramatic,
unexciting. It has to stir the heart in a long-disused way, it
has to awaken the intellect to a pleasure that ennobles and
wearies. I was at the first performance of an Ibsen play
given in England. It was *The Doll's House,* and at the fall
of the curtain I heard an old dramatic critic say, "It is but
a series of conversations terminated by an accident." So
far, we here in Dublin mean the same thing as do Mr.
Max Beerbohm, Mr. Walkley, and Mr. Archer, who are
seeking to restore sincerity to the English stage, but I am
not certain that we mean the same thing all through. The
utmost sincerity, the most unbroken logic, give me, at any
rate, but an imperfect pleasure if there is not a vivid and
beautiful language. Ibsen has sincerity and logic beyond
any writer of our time, and we are all seeking to learn them
at his hands; but is he not a good deal less than the greatest
of all times, because he lacks beautiful and vivid language?
"Well, well, give me time and you shall hear all about it. If
only I had Peter here now," is very like life, is entirely in
its place where it comes, and when it is united to other
sentences exactly like itself, one is moved, one knows

not how, to pity and terror, and yet not moved as if the words themselves could sing and shine. Mr. Max Beerbohm wrote once that a play cannot have style because the people must talk as they talk in daily life. He was thinking, it is obvious, of a play made out of that typically modern life where there is no longer vivid speech. Blake says that a work of art must be minutely articulated by God or man, and man has too little help from that occasional collaborateur when he writes of people whose language has become abstract and dead. Falstaff gives one the sensation of reality, and when one remembers the abundant vocabulary of a time when all but everything present to the mind was present to the senses, one imagines that his words were but little magnified from the words of such a man in real life. Language was still alive then, alive as it is in Gaelic today, as it is in English-speaking Ireland where the Schoolmaster or the newspaper has not corrupted it. I know that we are at the mere beginning, laboriously learning our craft, trying our hands in little plays for the most part, that we may not venture too boldly in our ignorance; but I never hear the vivid, picturesque, ever-varied language of Mr. Synge's persons without feeling that the great collaborateur has his finger in our business. May it not be that the only realistic play that will live as Shakespeare has lived, as Calderon has lived, as the Greeks have lived, will arise out of the common life, where language is as much alive as if it were new come out of Eden? After all, is not the greatest play, not the play that gives the sensation of an external reality, but the play in which there is the greatest abundance of life itself, of the reality that is in our minds? Is it possible to make a work of art, which needs every subtlety of expression if it is to reveal what hides itself continually, out of a dying, or at any rate a very ailing, language? and all language but that of the poets and of the poor is already bedridden. We have, indeed, persiflage, the only speech of educated men that expresses a deliberate enjoyment of words; but persiflage is not a true language. It is impersonal; it is not in the midst but on the edge of life; it covers more character than it discovers: and yet, such as it is, all our comedies are made out of it.

What the ever-moving, delicately molded flesh is to human beauty, vivid musical words are to passion. Somebody has said that every nation begins with poetry and ends with algebra, and passion has always refused to express itself in algebraical terms.

Have we not been in error in demanding from our playwrights personages who do not transcend our common actions any more than our common speech? If we are in the right, all antiquity has been in error. The scholars of a few generations ago were fond of deciding that certain persons were unworthy of the dignity of art. They had, it may be, an overabounding preference for kings and queens, but we are, it may be, very stupid in thinking that the average man is a fit subject at all for the finest art. Art delights in the exception, for it delights in the soul expressing itself according to its own laws and arranging the world about it in its own pattern, as sand strewn upon a drum will change itself into different patterns, according to the notes of music that are sung or played to it. But the average man is average because he has not attained to freedom. Habit, routine, fear of public opinion, fear of punishment here or hereafter, a myriad of things that are "something other than human life," something less than flame, work their will upon his soul and trundle his body here and there. At the first performance of *Ghosts* I could not escape from an illusion unaccountable to me at the time. All the characters seemed to be less than life-size; the stage, though it was but the little Royalty stage, seemed larger than I had ever seen it. Little whimpering puppets moved here and there in the middle of that great abyss. Why did they not speak out with louder voices or move with freer gestures? What was it that weighed upon their souls perpetually? Certainly they were all in prison, and yet there was no prison. In India there are villages so obedient that all the jailer has to do is to draw a circle upon the ground with his staff, and to tell his thief to stand there so many hours; but what law had these people broken that they had to wander round that narrow circle all their lives? May not such art, terrible, satirical, inhuman, be the medicine of great cities, where nobody is ever alone with his own strength? Nor is Maeterlinck very different, for his persons "inquire after Jerusalem in the regions of the grave with weak voices almost inarticulate, wearying repose." Is it the mob that has robbed those angelic persons of the energy of their souls? Will not our next art be rather of the country, of great open spaces, of the soul rejoicing in itself? Will not the generations to come begin again to have an overabounding faith in kings and queens, in masterful spirits, whatever names we call them by? I had Molière with me on my way to America, and as I read I seemed to be at home in Ireland listening to that conversation of the people which is so full of riches because so full of leisure, or to those old stories of the folk which were made by men who believed so much in the soul, and so little in anything else, that they were never entirely certain that the earth was solid under the foot-sole. What is there left for us, that have seen the newly discovered stability of things changed from an enthusiasm to a weariness, but to labor with a high heart, though it may be with weak hands, to rediscover an art of the theatre that shall be joyful, fantastic, extravagant, whimsical, beautiful, resonant, and altogether reckless? The arts are at their greatest when they seek for a life growing always more scornful of everything that is not itself and passing into its own fullness, as it were, ever more completely as all that is created out of the passing mode of society slips from it; and attaining that fullness, perfectly it may be—and from this is tragic joy and the perfectness of tragedy—when the world itself has slipped away in death. We, who are believers, cannot see reality anywhere but in the soul itself, and seeing it there we cannot do other than rejoice in every energy, whether of gesture, or of action, or of speech, coming out of the personality, the soul's image, even though the very laws of nature seem as unimportant in comparison as did the laws of Rome to Coriolanus when his pride was upon him. Has not the long decline of the arts been but the shadow of declining faith in an unseen reality?

> If the sun and moon would doubt,
> They'd immediately go out.

Men of letters have sometimes said that the characters of a romance or of a play must be typical. They mean that the character must be typical of something which exists in all men because the writer has found it in his own mind. It is one of the most inexplicable things about human nature that a writer, with a strange temperament, an Edgar Allan Poe, let us say, made what he is by conditions that never existed before, can create personages and lyric emotions, which startle us by being at once bizarre and an image of our own secret thoughts. Are we not face to face with the microcosm, mirroring everything in universal nature? It is no more necessary for the characters created by a romance writer, or a dramatist, to have existed before, than for his own personality to have done so; characters and personality alike, as is perhaps true in the instance of Poe, may draw half their life not from the solid earth but from some dreamy drug. This is true even of historical drama, for it was Goethe, the founder of the historical drama of Germany, who said: "We do the people of history the honor of naming after them the creations of our own minds." All that a dramatic writer need do is to persuade us, during the two hours' traffic of the stage, that the events of his play did really happen. He must know enough of the life of his country, or of history, to create this illusion, but no matter how much he knows he will fail if his audience is not ready to give up something of the dead letter. If his mind is full of energy he will not be satisfied with little knowledge, but he will be far more likely to alter incidents and characters, willfully even as it may seem, than to become a literal historian. It was one of the complaints against Shakespeare, in his own day, that he made Sir John Falstaff out of a praiseworthy old Lollard preacher. One day, as he sat over Holinshed's *History of England*, he persuaded himself that Richard the Second, with his French culture, "his too great friendliness to his friends," his beauty of mind, and his fall before dry, repelling Bolingbroke, would be a good image for an accustomed mood of fanciful, impracticable lyricism in his own mind. The historical Richard has passed away forever and the Richard of the play lives more intensely, it seems, than did ever living man. Yet Richard the Second, as Shakespeare made him, could never have been born before the Renaissance, before the Italian influence, or even one hour before the innumerable streams that flowed in upon Shakespeare's mind; the innumerable experiences we can never know, brought Shakespeare to the making of him. He is typical not because he ever existed, but because he has made us know of something in our minds we had never known of had he never been imagined.

Emotion of Multitude[3]

I have been thinking a good deal about plays lately,
and I have been wondering why I dislike the clear and
logical construction which seems necessary if one is to
succeed on the Modern Stage. It came into my head the
other day that this construction, which all the world has
learned from France, has everything of high literature
except the emotion of multitude. The Greek drama has
got the emotion of multitude from its chorus, which called
up famous sorrows, long-leaguered Troy, much-enduring
Odysseus, and all the gods and heroes to witness, as it were,
some well-ordered fable, some action separated but for
this from all but itself. The French play delights in the
well-ordered fable, but by leaving out the chorus it has
created an art where poetry and imagination, always the
children of far-off multitudinous things, must of necessity
grow less important than the mere will. This is why, I said
to myself, French dramatic poetry is so often a little
rhetorical, for rhetoric is the will trying to do the work
of the imagination. The Shakespearean Drama gets the
emotion of multitude out of the subplot which copies the
main plot, much as a shadow upon the wall copies one's
body in the firelight. We think of *King Lear* less as the
history of one man and his sorrows than as the history of
a whole evil time. Lear's shadow is in Gloster, who also
has ungrateful children, and the mind goes on imagining
other shadows, shadow beyond shadow till it has pictured
the world. In *Hamlet*, one hardly notices, so subtly is the
web woven, that the murder of Hamlet's father and the
sorrow of Hamlet are shadowed in the lives of Fortinbras
and Ophelia and Laertes, whose fathers, too, have been
killed. It is so in all the plays, or in all but all, and very
commonly the subplot is the main plot working itself out in
more ordinary men and women, and so doubly calling
up before us the image of multitude. Ibsen and Maeterlinck have on the other hand created a new form, for they
get multitude from the Wild Duck in the Attic, or from
the Crown at the bottom of the Fountain, vague symbols
that set the mind wandering from idea to idea, emotion to

[3] W. B. Yeats, "Emotion of Multitude," *Ideas of Good and
Evil* (London: A. H. Bullen, 1913), pp. 339–41.

emotion. Indeed all the great Masters have understood, that there cannot be great art without the little limited life of the fable, which is always the better the simpler it is, and the rich, far-wandering, many-imaged life of the half-seen world beyond it. There are some who understand that the simple unmysterious things living as in a clear noonlight are of the nature of the sun, and that vague many-imaged things have in them the strength of the moon. Did not the Egyptian carve it on emerald that all living things have the sun for father and the moon for mother, and has it not been said that a man of genius takes the most after his mother?

JOHN GALSWORTHY
(1867-1933)

Some Platitudes Concerning Drama[1] (1909)

A DRAMA must be shaped so as to have a spire of meaning. Every grouping of life and character has its inherent moral; and the business of the dramatist is so to pose the group as to bring that moral poignantly to the light of day. Such is the moral that exhales from plays like *Lear*, *Hamlet*, and *Macbeth*. But such is not the moral to be found in the great bulk of contemporary Drama. The moral of the average play is now, and probably has always been, the triumph at all costs of a supposed immediate ethical good over a supposed immediate ethical evil.

The vice of drawing these distorted morals has permeated the Drama to its spine; discolored its art, humanity, and significance; infected its creators, actors, audience, critics; too often turned it from a picture into a caricature. A Drama which lives under the shadow of the distorted moral forgets how to be free, fair, and fine—forgets so completely that it often prides itself on having forgotten.

Now, in writing plays, there are, in this matter of the moral, three courses open to the serious dramatist. The first is: To definitely set before the public that which it wishes to have set before it, the views and codes of life by which the public lives and in which it believes. This way is the most common, successful, and popular. It makes the dramatist's position sure, and not too obviously authoritative.

The second course is: To definitely set before the public those views and codes of life by which the dramatist himself lives, those theories in which he himself believes, the more effectively if they are the opposite of what the public wishes to have placed before it, presenting them so

[1] John Galsworthy, "Some Platitudes Concerning Drama," *The Inn of Tranquility: Studies and Essays* (New York: Charles Scribner's Sons, 1919), pp. 189–202.

that the audience may swallow them like powder in a spoonful of jam.

There is a third course: To set before the public no cut-and-dried codes, but the phenomena of life and character, selected and combined, *but not distorted,* by the dramatist's outlook, set down without fear, favor, or prejudice, leaving the public to draw such poor moral as nature may afford. This third method requires a certain detachment; it requires a sympathy with, a love of, and a curiosity as to, things for their own sake; it requires a far view, together with patient industry, for no immediately practical result.

It was once said of Shakespeare that he had never done any good to anyone, and never would. This, unfortunately, could not, in the sense in which the word "good" was then meant, be said of most modern dramatists. In truth, the good that Shakespeare did to humanity was of a remote, and, shall we say, eternal nature; something of the good that men get from having the sky and the sea to look at. And this partly because he was, in his greater plays at all events, free from the habit of drawing a distorted moral. Now, the playwright who supplies to the public the facts of life distorted by the moral which it expects, does so that he may do the public what he considers an immediate good, by fortifying its prejudices; and the dramatist who supplies to the public facts distorted by his own advanced morality, does so because he considers that he will at once benefit the public by substituting for its worn-out ethics, his own. In both cases the advantage the dramatist hopes to confer on the public is immediate and practical.

But matters change, and morals change; men remain —and to set men, and the facts about them, down faithfully, so that they draw for us the moral of their natural actions, may also possibly be of benefit to the community. It is, at all events, harder then to set men and facts down, as they ought, or ought not to be. This, however, is not to say that a dramatist should, or indeed can, keep himself and his temperamental philosophy out of his work. As a man lives and thinks, so will he write. But it is certain, that to the making of good drama, as to the practice of every other art, there must be brought an almost passionate love of discipline, a white heat of self-respect, a desire to make the truest, fairest, best thing in one's power; and that to these must be added an eye that does not flinch. Such qualities alone will bring to a drama the selfless character which soaks it with inevitability.

The word "pessimist" is frequently applied to the few dramatists who have been content to work in this way. It has been applied, among others, to Euripides, to Shakespeare, to Ibsen; it will be applied to many in the future. Nothing, however, is more dubious than the way in which these two words "pessimist" and "optimist" are used; for the optimist appears to be he who cannot bear the world as it is, and is forced by his nature to picture it as it ought to be, and the pessimist one who cannot only bear the world as it is, but loves it well enough to draw it faithfully. The true lover of the human race is surely he who can put up with it in all its forms, in vice as well as in virtue, in defeat no less than in victory; the true seer he who sees not only joy but sorrow, the true painter of human life one who blinks at nothing. It may be that he is also, incidentally, its true benefactor.

In the whole range of the social fabric there are only two impartial persons, the scientist and the artist, and under the latter heading such dramatists as desire to write not only for today, but for tomorrow, must strive to come.

But dramatists being as they are made—past remedy— it is perhaps more profitable to examine the various points at which their qualities and defects are shown.

The plot! A good plot is that sure edifice which slowly rises out of the interplay of circumstance on temperament, and temperament on circumstance, within the enclosing atmosphere of an idea. A human being is the best plot there is; it may be impossible to see why he is a good plot, because the idea within which he was brought forth cannot be fully grasped; but it is plain that *he is a good plot.* He is organic. And so it must be with a good play. Reason alone produces no good plots; they come by original sin, sure conception, and instinctive after-power of selecting what benefits the germ. A bad plot, on the other hand, is simply a row of stakes, with a character impaled on each— characters who would have liked to live, but came to untimely grief; who started bravely, but fell on these stakes, placed beforehand in a row, and were transfixed one by one, while their ghosts stride on, squeaking and gibbering, through the play. Whether these stakes are made of facts or of ideas, according to the nature of the dramatist who planted them, their effect on the unfortunate characters is the same; the creatures were begotten to be staked, and staked they are! The demand for a good plot, not unfrequently heard, commonly signifies: "Tickle my sensations by stuffing the play with arbitrary adventures, so that I need not be troubled to take the characters seriously. Set the persons of the play to action, regardless of time, sequence, atmosphere, and probability!"

Now, true dramatic action is what characters do, at once contrary, as it were, to expectation, and yet because they have already done other things. No dramatist should let his audience know what is coming; but neither should he suffer his characters to act without making his audience feel that those actions are in harmony with temperament, and arise from previous known actions, together with the temperaments and previous known actions of the other characters in the play. The dramatist who hangs his characters to his plot, instead of hanging his plot to his characters, is guilty of cardinal sin.

The dialogue! Good dialogue again is character, marshaled so as continually to stimulate interest or excitement. The reason good dialogue is seldom found in plays is merely that it is hard to write, for it requires not only a knowledge of what interests or excites, but such a feeling for character as brings misery to the dramatist's heart when his creations speak as they should not speak—ashes to his mouth when they say things for the sake of saying them—disgust when they are "smart."

The art of writing true dramatic dialogue is an austere art, denying itself all license, grudging every sentence devoted to the mere machinery of the play, suppressing all jokes and epigrams severed from character, relying for fun and pathos on the fun and tears of life. From start to finish good dialogue is handmade, like good lace; clear, of fine texture, furthering with each thread the harmony and strength of a design to which all must be subordinated.

But good dialogue is also spiritual action. In so far as the dramatist divorces his dialogue from spiritual action —that is to say, from progress of events, or toward events which are significant of character—he is stultifying $\tau\grave{o}$ $\delta\rho\acute{a}\mu a$ the thing done; he may make pleasing disquisitions, he is not making drama. And in so far as he twists character to suit his moral or his plot, he is neglecting a first principle, that truth to Nature which alone invests art with handmade quality.

The dramatist's license, in fact, ends with his design. In conception alone he is free. He may take what character or group of characters he chooses, see them with what eyes, knit them with what idea, within the limits of his temperament; but once taken, seen, and knitted, he is bound to treat them like a gentleman, with the tenderest consideration of their mainsprings. Take care of character; action and dialogue will take care of themselves! The true dramatist gives full rein to his temperament in the scope and nature of his subject; having once selected subject and characters, he is just, gentle, restrained, neither gratifying his lust for praise at the expense of his offspring, nor using them as puppets to flout his audience. Being himself the nature that brought them forth, he guides them in the course predestined at their conception. So only have they a chance of defying Time, which is always lying in wait to destroy the false, topical, or fashionable, all—in a word—that is not based on the permanent elements of human nature. The perfect dramatist rounds up his characters and facts within the ring-fence of a dominant idea which fulfills the craving of his spirit; having got them there, he suffers them to live their own lives.

Plot, action, character, dialogue! But there is yet another subject for a platitude. Flavor! An impalpable quality, less easily captured than the scent of a flower, the peculiar and most essential attribute of any work of art! It is the thin, poignant spirit which hovers up out of a play, and is as much its differentiating essence as is caffeine of coffee. Flavor, in fine, is the spirit of the dramatist projected into his work in a state of volatility, so that no one can exactly lay hands on it, here, there, or anywhere. This distinctive essence of a play, marking its brand, is the one thing at which the dramatist cannot work, for it is outside his consciousness. A man may have many moods, he has but one spirit; and this spirit he communicates in some subtle, unconscious way to all his work. It waxes and wanes with the currents of his vitality, but no more alters than a chestnut changes into an oak.

For, in truth, dramas are very like unto trees, springing from seedlings, shaping themselves inevitably in accordance with the laws fast hidden within themselves, drinking sustenance from the earth and air, and in conflict with the natural forces round them. So they slowly come to full growth, until warped, stunted, or risen to fair and gracious

height, they stand open to all the winds. And the trees that
spring from each dramatist are of different race; he is
the spirit of his own sacred grove, into which no stray
tree can by any chance enter.

One more platitude. It is not unfashionable to pit one
form of drama against another—holding up the naturalistic
to the disadvantage of the epic; the epic to the be-
littlement of the fantastic; the fantastic to the detriment
of the naturalistic. Little purpose is thus served. The
essential meaning, truth, beauty, and irony of things may be
revealed under all these forms. Vision over life and human
nature can be as keen and just, the revelation as true,
inspiring, delight-giving, and thought-provoking, whatever
fashion be employed—it is simply a question of doing it
well enough to uncover the kernel of the nut. Whether the
violet come from Russia, from Parma, or from England,
matters little. Close by the Greek temples at Paestum there
are violets that seem redder, and sweeter, than any ever
seen—as though they have sprung up out of the footprints
of some old pagan goddess; but under the April sun, in a
Devonshire lane, the little blue scentless violets capture
every bit as much of the spring. And so it is with drama—
no matter what its form—it need only be the "real thing,"
need only have caught some of the precious fluids, revelation, or delight, and imprisoned them within a chalice to
which we may put our lips and continually drink.

And yet, starting from this last platitude, one may
perhaps be suffered to speculate as to the particular
forms that our renascent drama is likely to assume. For
our drama is renascent, and nothing will stop its growth.
It is not renascent because this or that man is writing, but
because of a new spirit. A spirit that is no doubt in part
the gradual outcome of the impact on our home-grown
art, of Russian, French, and Scandinavian influences, but
which in the main rises from an awakened humanity in the
conscience of our time.

What, then, are to be the main channels down which
the renascent English drama will float in the coming years?
It is more than possible that these main channels will come
to be two in number and situate far apart.

The one will be the broad and clear-cut channel of
naturalism, down which will course a drama poignantly
shaped, and inspired with high intention, but faithful to
the seething and multiple life around us, drama such as

some are inclined to term photographic, deceived by a seeming simplicity into forgetfulness of the old proverb, "*Ars est celare artem*," and oblivious of the fact that, to be vital, to grip, such drama is in every respect as dependent on imagination, construction, selection, and elimination—the main laws of artistry—as ever was the romantic or rhapsodic play. The question of naturalistic technique will bear, indeed, much more study than has yet been given to it. The aim of the dramatist employing it is obviously to create such an illusion of actual life passing on the stage as to compel the spectator to pass through an experience of his own, to think, and talk, and move with the people he sees thinking, talking, and moving in front of him. A false phrase, a single word out of tune or time, will destroy that illusion and spoil the surface as surely as a stone heaved into a still pool shatters the image seen there. But this is only the beginning of the reason why the naturalistic is the most exacting and difficult of all techniques. It is easy enough to *reproduce* the exact conversation and movements of persons in a room; it is desperately hard to *produce* the perfectly natural conversation and movements of those persons, when each natural phrase spoken and each natural movement made has not only to contribute toward the growth and perfection of a drama's soul, but also to be a revelation, phrase by phrase, movement by movement, of essential traits of character. To put it another way, naturalistic art, when alive, indeed to be alive at all, is simply the art of manipulating a procession of most delicate symbols. Its service is the swaying and focusing of men's feelings and thought in the various departments of human life. It will be like a steady lamp, held up from time to time, in whose light things will be seen for a space clearly and in due proportion, freed from the mists of prejudice and partisanship.

And the other of these two main channels will, I think, be a twisting and delicious stream, which will bear on its breast new barques of poetry, shaped, it may be, like prose, but a prose incarnating through its fantasy and symbolism all the deeper aspirations, yearning, doubts, and mysterious stirrings of the human spirit; a poetic prose drama, emotionalizing us by its diversity and purity of form and invention, and whose province will be to disclose the elemental soul of man and the forces of Nature, not perhaps as the old tragedies disclosed them, not necessarily in the epic mood, but always with beauty and in the spirit of discovery.

Such will, I think be the two vital forms of our drama in the coming generation. And between these two forms there must be no crude unions; they are too far apart, the cross is too violent. For, where there is a seeming blend of lyricism and naturalism, it will on examination be found, I think, to exist only in plays whose subjects or settings—as in Synge's *Playboy of the Western World,* or in Mr. Masefield's *Nan*—are so removed from our ken that we cannot really tell, and therefore do not care, whether an absolute illusion is maintained. The poetry which may and should exist in naturalistic drama, can only be that of perfect rightness of proportion, rhythm, shape—the poetry, in fact, that lies in all vital things. It is the ill-mating of forms that has killed a thousand plays. We want no more bastard drama; no more attempts to dress out the simple dignity of everyday life in the peacock's feathers of false lyricism; no more straw-stuffed heroes or heroines; no more rabbits and goldfish from the conjurer's pockets, nor any limelight. Let us have starlight, moonlight, sunlight, and the light of our own self-respects.

BERNARD SHAW
(1856-1950)

How to Write a Popular Play[1] (1909)

... THE FORMULA for the well made play is so easy that I give it for the benefit of any reader who feels tempted to try his hand at making the fortune that awaits all successful manufacturers in this line. First, you "have an idea" for a dramatic situation. If it strikes you as a splendidly original idea, whilst it is in fact as old as the hills, so much the better. For instance, the situation of an innocent person convicted by circumstances of a crime may always be depended on. If the person is a woman, she must be convicted of adultery. If a young officer, he must be convicted of selling information to the enemy, though it is really a fascinating female spy who has ensnared him and stolen the incriminating document. If the innocent wife, banished from her home, suffers agonies through her separation from her children, and, when one of them is dying (of any disease the dramatist chooses to inflict), disguises herself as a nurse and attends it through its dying convulsion until the doctor, who should be a serio-comic character, and if possible a faithful old admirer of the lady's, simultaneously announces the recovery of the child and the discovery of the wife's innocence, the success of the play may be regarded as assured if the writer has any sort of knack for his work. Comedy is more difficult, because it requires a sense of humor and a good deal of vivacity; but the process is essentially the same: it is the manufacture of a misunderstanding. Having manufactured it, you place its culmination at the end of the last act but one, which is the point at which the manufacture of the play begins. Then you make your first act out of the necessary introduction of the characters to the audience, after

[1] George Bernard Shaw, Preface, *Three Plays by Brieux* (New York: Brentano's, 1911), pp. xxii–xxvii. Reprinted by permission of The Public Trustee and The Society of Authors.

elaborate explanations, mostly conducted by servants, so-
licitors, and other low life personages (the principals must
all be dukes and colonels and millionaires), of how the
misunderstanding is going to come about. Your last act
consists, of course, of clearing up the misunderstanding,
and generally getting the audience out of the theatre as
best you can.

Now please do not misunderstand me as pretending
that this process is so mechanical that it offers no opportunity for the exercise of talent. On the contrary, it is
so mechanical that without very conspicuous talent nobody
can make much reputation by doing it, though some can
and do make a living at it. And this often leads the
cultivated classes to suppose that all plays are written by
authors of talent. As a matter of fact the majority of
those who in France and England make a living by writing
plays are unknown and, as to education, all but illiterate.
Their names are not worth putting on the playbill, because
their audiences neither know nor care who the author is, and
often believe that the actors improvise the whole piece, just
as they in fact do sometimes improvise the dialogue. To
rise out of this obscurity you must be a Scribe or a Sardou,
doing essentially the same thing, it is true, but doing it
wittily and ingeniously, at moments almost poetically,
and giving the persons of the drama some touches of real
observed character.

WHY THE CRITICS ARE ALWAYS WRONG

Now it is these strokes of talent that set the critics
wrong. For the talent, being all expended on the formula,
at least consecrates the formula in the eyes of the critics.
Nay, they become so accustomed to the formula that at
last they cannot relish or understand a play that has
grown naturally, just as they cannot admire the Venus
of Milo because she has neither a corset nor high heeled
shoes. They are like the peasants who are so accustomed to
food reeking with garlic that when food is served to them
without it they declare that it has no taste and is not food
at all.

This is the explanation of the refusal of the critics of
all nations to accept great original dramatists like Ibsen
and Brieux as real dramatists, or their plays as real
plays. No writer of the first order needs the formula any

more than a sound man needs a crutch. In his simplest mood, when he is only seeking to amuse, he does not manufacture a plot: he tells a story. He finds no difficulty in setting people on the stage to talk and act in an amusing, exciting or touching way. His characters have adventures and ideas which are interesting in themselves, and need not be fitted into the Chinese puzzle of a plot.

THE INTERPRETER OF LIFE

But the great dramatist has something better to do than to amuse either himself or his audience. He has to interpret life. This sounds a mere pious phrase of literary criticism; but a moment's consideration will discover its meaning and its exactitude. Life as it appears to us in our daily experience is an unintelligible chaos of happenings. You pass Othello in the bazaar in Aleppo, Iago on the jetty in Cyprus, and Desdemona in the nave of St. Mark's in Venice without the slightest clue to their relations to one another. The man you see stepping into a chemist's shop to buy the means of committing murder or suicide, may, for all you know, want nothing but a liver pill or a tooth-brush. The statesman who has no other object than to make you vote for his party at the next election, may be starting you on an incline at the foot of which lies war, or revolution, or a smallpox epidemic or five years off your lifetime. The horrible murder of a whole family by the father who finishes by killing himself, or the driving of a young girl on to the streets, may be the result of your discharging an employee in a fit of temper a month before. To attempt to understand life from merely looking on at it as it happens in the streets is as hopeless as trying to understand public questions by studying snapshots of public demonstrations. If we possessed a series of cinematographs of all the executions during the Reign of Terror, they might be exhibited a thousand times without enlightening the audiences in the least as to the meaning of the Revolution: Robespierre would perish as "un monsieur" and Marie Antoinette as "une femme." Life as it occurs is senseless: a policeman may watch it and work in it for thirty years in the streets and courts of Paris without learning as much of it or from it as a child or a nun may learn from a single play by Brieux. For it is the business of Brieux to pick out the significant incidents from the chaos of daily happenings, and arrange them so that their relation to one another becomes significant, thus changing us from bewildered spectators of a monstrous confusion to men intelligently conscious of the world and its destinies. This is the highest function that man can perform—the greatest work he can set his hand to; and this is why the great dramatists of the world, from Euripides and Aristophanes to Shakespear and Molière, and from them to Ibsen and Brieux, take that majestic and pontifical rank which seems so strangely above all the reasonable pretensions of mere strolling actors and theatrical authors.

HOW THE GREAT DRAMATISTS TORTURE THE PUBLIC

Now if the critics are wrong in supposing that the formula of the well made play is not only an indispensable factor in playwriting, but is actually the essence of the play itself —if their delusion is rebuked and confuted by the practice of every great dramatist, even when he is only amusing himself by story telling, what must happen to their poor formula when it impertinently offers its services to a playwright who has taken on his supreme function as the Interpreter of Life? Not only has he no use for it, but he must attack and destroy it; for one of the very first lessons he has to teach to a play-ridden public is that the romantic conventions on which the formula proceeds are all false, and are doing incalculable harm in these days when everybody reads romances and goes to the theatre. Just as the historian can teach no real history until he has cured his readers of the romantic delusion that the greatness of a queen consists in her being a pretty woman and having her head cut off, so the playwright of the first order can do nothing with his audiences until he has cured them of looking at the stage through the keyhole, and sniffing round the theatre as prurient people sniff round the divorce court. The cure is not a popular one. The public suffers from it exactly as a drunkard or a snuff taker suffers from an attempt to conquer the habit. The critics especially, who are forced by their profession to indulge immoderately in plays adulterated with falsehood and vice, suffer so acutely when deprived of them for a whole evening that they hurl disparagements and even abuse and insult at the merciless dramatist who is torturing them. To a bad play of the kind they are accustomed to they can be cruel through superciliousness, irony, impatience, contempt, or even a Rochefoucauldian pleasure in a friend's misfortune. But the hatred provoked by deliberately inflicted pain, the frantic denials as of a prisoner at the bar accused of a disgraceful crime, the clamor for vengeance thinly disguised as artistic justice, the suspicion that the dramatist is using private information and making a personal attack: all these are to be found only when the playwright is no mere *marchand de plaisir*, but, like Brieux, a ruthless revealer of hidden truth and a mighty destroyer of idols.

FEDERICO GARCÍA LORCA
(1899-1936)

The Authority of the Theatre[1] (1934)

MY DEAR FRIENDS: Some time ago I made a solemn promise to refuse every kind of tribute, banquet, or celebration which might be made in my honor, first, because I know that each of them drives another nail into our literary coffin, and second, because I have found that there is nothing more depressing than a formal speech made in our honor, and nothing sadder than organized applause, however sincere.

Besides, between ourselves, I hold that banquets and scrolls bring bad luck upon the one who receives them, bad luck springing from the relief of his friends who think: "Now we have done our duty by him."

A banquet is a gathering of professional people who eat with us, and where we find thrown together every kind of person who likes us least.

Rather than do honor to poets and dramatists, I should prepare challenges and attacks, in which we should be told roundly and passionately: "Are you afraid of doing this?" "Are you incapable of expressing a person's anguish at the sea?" "Daren't you show the despair of soldiers who hate war?"

Necessity and struggle, grounded on a critical love, temper the artist's soul, which easy flattery makes effeminate and destroys. The theatres are full of deceiving sirens, garlanded with hothouse roses, and the public is content, and applauds dummy hearts and superficial dialogue; but the dramatic poet who wishes to save himself from oblivion must not forget the open fields with their wild roses, fields moistened by the dawn where peasants toil,

[1] Federico García Lorca, "The Prophecy of Lorca," translated by Albert E. Sloman, *Theatre Arts*, October, 1950, pp. 38–39. Reprinted by courtesy of Francisco García Lorca and Albert E. Sloman. This address was delivered after the opening of *Yerma*.

and the pigeon, wounded by a mysterious hunter, which is dying amongst the rushes with no one to hear its grief.

Shunning sirens, flattery, and congratulations, I have accepted nothing in my honor, on the occasion of the first night of *Yerma*; but it has been the greatest pleasure of my short life as a writer to learn that the theatre world of Madrid was asking the great Margarita Xirgu, an actress with an impeccable artistic career, luminary of the Spanish theatre, and admirable interpreter of the part of Yerma, together with the company which so brilliantly supports her, for a special production.

For the interest and attention in a notable theatrical endeavor which this implies, I wish, now that we are all together, to give to you my deepest and sincerest thanks. I am not speaking tonight as an author, nor as a poet, nor as a simple student of the rich panorama of man's life, but as an ardent lover of the theatre of social action. The theatre is one of the most useful and expressive instruments for a country's edification, the barometer which registers its greatness or its decline. A theatre which in every branch, from tragedy to vaudeville, is sensitive and well oriented, can in a few years change the sensibility of a people, and a broken-down theatre, where wings have given way to cloven hoofs, can coarsen and benumb a whole nation.

The theatre is a school of weeping and of laughter, a rostrum where men are free to expose old and equivocal standards of conduct, and explain with living examples the eternal norms of the heart and feelings of man.

A nation which does not help and does not encourage its theatre is, if not dead, dying; just as the theatre which does not feel the social pulse, the historical pulse, the drama of its people, and catch the genuine color of its landscape and of its spirit, with laughter or with tears, has no right to call itself a theatre, but an amusement hall, or a place for doing that dreadful thing known as "killing time." I am referring to no one, and I want to offend no one; I am not speaking of actual fact, but of a problem that has yet to be solved.

Every day, my friends, I hear about the crisis in the theatre, and I feel always that the defect is not one before our eyes, but deep down in its very nature; it is not a defect of the flower we have before us, of a play, that is, but deeply rooted; in short, a defect of organization. Whilst

actors and authors are in the hands of managements that
are completely commercial, free, without either literary or
state control of any kind, managements devoid of all
judgment and offering no kind of safeguard, actors, authors,
and the whole theatre will sink lower every day, beyond all
hope of salvation.

The delightful light theatre of revue, vaudeville, and
farce, forms of which I am a keen spectator, could maintain and even save itself; but plays in verse, the historical
play, and the so-called Spanish *zarzuela*, will suffer more
and more setbacks, because they are forms which make
great demands and which admit of real innovations, and
there is neither the authority nor the spirit of sacrifice to
impose them on a public which has to be overruled from
above, and often contradicted and attacked. The theatre
must impose itself on the public, not the public on the
theatre. To do this, authors and actors must, whatever the
cost, again assume great authority, because the theatre-
going public is like a school child; it reveres the stern,
severe teacher who demands justice and sees justice done;
and puts pins on the chairs of the timid and flattering
ones who neither teach themselves nor allow anyone else to
teach.

The public can be taught—I say public, of course, not
people—it can be taught; for, some years ago, I saw
Debussy and Ravel howled down, and I have been present
since at loud ovations given by a public of ordinary people
to the very works which were earlier rejected. These
authors were imposed by the high judgment of authority,
superior to that of the ordinary public, just as were
Wedekind in Germany and Pirandello in Italy, and so
many others.

This has to be done for the good of the theatre and for
the glory and status of its interpreters. Dignity must be
maintained, in the conviction that such dignity will be
amply repaid. To do otherwise is to tremble behind the
flies, and kill the fantasies, imagination, and charm of the
theatre, which is always, always an art, and will always be a
lofty art, even though there may have been a time when
everything which pleased was labeled art, so that the tone
was lowered, poetry destroyed, and the stage itself a
refuge for thieves.

Art above all else. A most noble art, and you, my actor
friends, artists above all else. Artists from head to foot,

since through love and vocation you have risen to the make-believe and pitiful world of the boards. Artists by occupation and by preoccupation. From the smallest theatre to the most eminent, the word "Art" should be written in auditoriums and dressing rooms, for if not we shall have to write the word "Commerce" or some other that I dare not say. And distinction, discipline, and sacrifice and love.

I don't want to lecture you, because I should be the one receiving a lecture. My words are dictated by enthusiasm and conviction. I labor under no delusion. As a good Andalusian I can think coolly, because I come of an ancient stock. I know that truth does not lie with him who says, "Today, today, today," eating his bread close to the hearth, but with him who watches calmly at a distance the first light of dawn in the country.

I know that those people who say, "Now, now, now," with their eyes fixed on the small jaws of the box office are not right, but those who say, "Tomorrow, tomorrow, tomorrow," and feel the approach of the new life which is hovering over the world.

Two Laws[1]

TWO LAWS govern—if I may thus express myself—the eternal status of the playwright.

The first law defines the sad and slightly ridiculous position of the playwright toward those of his characters he has created and given to the theatre. Just as a character, before being played by an actor, is docile toward the author, familiar, and a part of him—as you may judge from my own creations—so once he appears before the audience he becomes a stranger and indifferent. The first actor who plays him represents the first in a series of reincarnations by which the character draws further and further away from his creator and escapes him forever.

In fact, this is true of the play in its entirety. From the first performance on, it belongs to the actors. The author wandering in the wings is a kind of ghost whom the stagehands detest if he listens in or is indiscreet. After the hundredth performance, particularly if it is a good play, it belongs to the public. In reality the only thing the playwright can call his own is his bad plays. The independence of those of his characters who have succeeded is complete: the life they lead on road tours or in America is a constant denial of their filial obligations. So while the hero of your novels follows you everywhere, calling you "father" or "papa," those of your stage characters you chance to meet—as I have—in Carcassonne or Los Angeles, have become total strangers to you.

It was largely to punish them for this independence that Goethe, Claudel, and so many other writers wrote a new version for their favorite heroines—but in vain. The new Marguerite, the new Hélène, or the new Violaine left

[1] Jean Giraudoux, *Visitations* (Neuchâtel and Paris: Ides et Calendes) pp. 121–28. Reprinted by courtesy of Jean-Pierre Giraudoux.

their creators just as quickly. Once I was at a performance of Claudel's *Tidings Brought to Mary*. That day, at least, this law operated in my favor: I noted that the play belonged more to me than to Claudel.

How many playwrights are forced to seek in an actor or actress the memory or reflection of their sons and daughters who have escaped; just as, in daily life, other parents look for the same thing in a son-in-law or daughter-in-law. . . . On the terrace of the Café Weber, in the lobby during a dress rehearsal, on the lawn of the country house of a noted actress, how often we have met such couples: Feydeau and Mme. Cassive, Jules Renard and Suzanne Desprez, Maurice Donnay and Réjane. The woman slightly inattentive, the man alert, reminiscing, chatty, full of questions, was talking of his absent "child."

The second law, a corollary and inverse of the first, defines the wonderful position of the playwright toward his era and its events, and indicates his role therein. Here, if I wish to be sincere, I must strip myself and my colleagues of all false modesty. The figure who in the play is merely a voice, without personality, without responsibility, implacable, but a historian and an avenger, exists in a given era in flesh and blood: the playwright himself. Of all writers in the theatre worthy of the name, one should be able to say, when they appear: Add the archangel! It is futile to believe that a year or a century can find the resonance and elevation ultimately befitting the emotional debate and effort represented by each period of our passage on earth, if it does not have a spokesman of its tragedy or drama in order to reach its heights or plumb its depths. Tragedy and drama are the confession which humanity— this army of salvation and ruin—must also make in public, without reticence and in loudest tones, for the echo of its voice is clearer and more real than its voice itself. Make no mistake about it. The relationship between the theatre and religious ceremonial is obvious; it is no accident that in former times plays were given on all occasions in front of our cathedrals. The theatre is most at home on the open space in front of a church. That is what the audience goes to, on gala evenings in the theatre: toward the illuminated confession of its petty and giant destinies.

Calderon is humanity confessing its thirst for eternity, Corneille its dignity, Racine its weakness, Shakespeare its appetite for life, Claudel its state of sin and salvation, Goethe its humanity, Kleist its vividness. Epochs have not come to terms with themselves unless crowds, dressed in their most striking costumes of confession, so as to increase the solemnity of the occasion, come to these radiant confessionals called theatres and arenas, to listen to their own avowals of cowardice and sacrifice, hatred and passion. And unless they also cry: Add the prophet!

For there is no theatre save that of divination. Not that false divination which gives names and dates, but the real thing: the one which reveals to men these amazing truths—that the living must live, that the living must die, that autumn follows summer, spring follows winter, that there are four elements, happiness, millions of catastrophes, that life is a reality, that it is a dream, that man lives by peace, that man lives by blood; in short, what they will never know.

That is theatre: the public recall of those incredible splendors whose visions disturb and overwhelm audiences by night. But—and this it is which heartens me—already by dawn the lesson and the memory are diluted, no doubt in order to make the writer's mission a daily one. Of such is the performance of a play: the sudden awareness in the spectator of the permanent state of this living and indifferent humanity—passion and death.

Translated by Joseph M. Bernstein

EUGENE O'NEILL
(1888-1953)

Memoranda on Masks[1] (1932)

NOT MASKS for all plays, naturally. Obviously not for plays
conceived in purely realistic terms. But masks for certain
types of plays, especially for the new modern play, as yet
only dimly foreshadowed in a few groping specimens, but
which must inevitably be written in the future. For I hold
more and more surely to the conviction that the use of
masks will be discovered eventually to be the freest solution
of the modern dramatist's problem as to how—with the
greatest possible dramatic clarity and economy of means
—he can express those profound hidden conflicts of the
mind which the probings of psychology continue to disclose
to us. He must find some method to present this inner
drama in his work, or confess himself incapable of por-
traying one of the most characteristic preoccupations and
uniquely significant, spiritual impulses of his time. With his
old—and more than a bit senile!—standby of realistic
technique, he can do no more than, at best, obscurely hint
at it through a realistically disguised surface symbolism,
superficial and misleading. But that, while sufficiently be-
guiling to the sentimentally mystical, is hardly enough. A
comprehensive expression is demanded here, a chance for
eloquent presentation, a new form of drama projected from
a fresh insight into the inner forces motivating the actions
and reactions of men and women (a new and truer
characterization, in other words)—a drama of souls, and
the adventures of "free wills," with the masks that govern
them and constitute their fates.

For what, at bottom, is the new psychological insight
into human cause and effect but a study in masks, an
exercise in unmasking? Whether we think the attempted

[1] Eugene O'Neill, "Memoranda on Masks," *The American
Spectator,* November, 1932, p. 3. The *American Spectator*
articles reprinted by courtesy of Mrs. Carlotta Monterey O'Neill.

unmasking has been successful, or has only created for
itself new masks, is of no importance here. What is valid,
what is unquestionable, is that this insight has uncovered
the mask, has impressed the idea of mask as a symbol of
inner reality upon all intelligent people of today; and I
know they would welcome the use of masks in the theatre as
a necessary, dramatically revealing new convention, and
not regard them as any "stunty" resurrection of archaic
props.

This was strikingly demonstrated for me in practical experience by *The Great God Brown,* which ran in New York
for eight months, nearly all of that time in Broadway
theatres—a play in which the use of masks was an integral
part of the theme. There was some misunderstanding, of
course. But so is there always misunderstanding in the
case of every realistic play that attempts to express anything beyond what is contained in a human-interest newspaper story. In the main, however, *The Great God Brown*
was accepted and appreciated by both critics and public—
a fairly extensive public, as its run gives evidence.

I emphasize this play's success because the fact that a
mask drama, the main values of which are psychological,
mystical, and abstract, could be played in New York for
eight months, has always seemed to me a more significant
proof of the deeply responsive possibilities in our public
than anything that has happened in our modern theatre before or since.

(2)

Looked at from even the most practical standpoint of
the practicing playwright, the mask *is* dramatic in itself,
has always been dramatic in itself, *is* a proven weapon of
attack. At its best, it is more subtly, imaginatively, sug-
gestively dramatic than any actor's face can ever be. Let
anyone who doubts this study the Japanese Noh masks, or
Chinese theatre masks, or African primitive masks—or
right here in America the faces of the big marionettes
Robert Edmond Jones made for the production of Stra-
vinsky's *Oedipus,* or Benda's famous masks, or even photographs of them.

(3)

Dogma for the new masked drama. One's outer life passes in a solitude haunted by the masks of others; one's inner life passes in a solitude hounded by the masks of oneself.

(4)

With masked mob a new type of play may be written in which the Mob as King, Hero, Villain, or Fool will be the main character—The Great Democratic Play!

(5)

Why not give all future Classical revivals entirely in masks? *Hamlet,* for example. Masks would liberate this play from its present confining status as exclusively a "star vehicle." We would be able to see the great drama we are now only privileged to read, to identify ourselves with the figure of Hamlet as a symbolic projection of a fate that is in each of us, instead of merely watching a star giving us his version of a great acting role. We would even be able to hear the sublime poetry as the innate expression of the spirit of the drama itself, instead of listening to it as realistic recitation—or ranting—by familiar actors.

(6)

Consider Goethe's *Faust,* which, psychologically speaking, should be the closest to us of all the Classics. In producing this play, I would have Mephistopheles wearing the Mephistophelean mask of the face of Faust. For is not the whole of Goethe's truth *for our time* just that Mephistopheles and Faust are one and the same—*are* Faust?

Second Thoughts[2] (1932)

What would I change in past productions of my plays if I could live through them again? Many things. In some plays, considerable revision of the writing of some of the

[2] Eugene O'Neill, "Second Thoughts," *The American Spectator,* December, 1932, p. 2.

scenes would strike me as imperative. Other plays—*The First Man, Gold, Welded, The Fountain*—I would dismiss as being too painfully bungled in their present form to be worth producing at all.

But one thing I most certainly would not change: the use of masks in *The Hairy Ape,* in my arrangement of Coleridge's "Ancient Mariner," in *All God's Chillun Got Wings* (the symbol of the African primitive mask in the last part of the play, which, in the production in Russian by the Moscow Kamerny Theatre I saw in Paris, is dramatically intensified and emphasized), in *The Great God Brown* and, finally, in *Lazarus Laughed,* in which all the characters except Lazarus remain masked throughout the play. I regard this use of masks as having been uniformly successful.

The change I would make would be to call for more masks in some of these productions and to use them in other productions where they were not used before. In *The Emperor Jones,* for example. All the figures in Jones's flight through the forest should be masked. Masks would dramatically stress their phantasmal quality, as contrasted with the unmasked Jones, intensify the supernatural menace of the tomtom, give the play a more complete and vivid expression. In *The Hairy Ape* a much more extensive use of masks would be of the greatest value in emphasizing the theme of the play. From the opening of the fourth scene, where Yank begins to think, he enters into a masked world; even the familiar faces of his mates in the forecastle have become strange and alien. They should be masked, and the faces of everyone he encounters thereafter, including the symbolic gorilla's.

In *All God's Chillun Got Wings,* all save the seven leading characters should be masked; for all the secondary figures are part and parcel of the Expressionistic background of the play, a world at first indifferent, then cruelly hostile, against which the tragedy of Jim Harris is outlined. In *The Great God Brown* I would now make the masks symbolize more definitely the abstract theme of the play instead of, as in the old production, stressing the more superficial meaning that people wear masks before other people and are mistaken by them for their masks.

In *Marco Millions* all the people of the East should be masked—Kublai, the Princess Kokachin, all of them! For anyone who has been in the East, or who has read

Eastern philosophy, the reason for this is obvious. It is an exact dramatic expression of West confronted by East. Morever, it is the only possible way to project this contrast truthfully in the theatre, for Western actors cannot convey Eastern character realistically, and their only chance to suggest it convincingly is with the help of masks.

As for *Strange Interlude,* that is an attempt at the new masked psychological drama which I have discussed before, without masks—a successful attempt, perhaps, in so far as it concerns only surfaces and their immediate subsurfaces, but not where, occasionally, it tries to probe deeper.

With *Mourning Becomes Electra,* masks were called for in one draft of the three plays. But the Classical connotation was too insistent. Masks in that connection demand great language to speak—which let me out of it with a sickening bump! So I had to discard them. There was a realistic New England insistence in my mind, too, which would have barred great language even in a dramatist capable of writing it, an insistence on the clotted and clogged and inarticulate. So it evolved ultimately into the "masklike faces," which expressed my intention tempered by the circumstances. However, I should like to see *Mourning Becomes Electra* done entirely with masks, now that I can view it solely as a psychological play, quite removed from the confusing preoccupations the Classical derivation of its plot once caused me. Masks would emphasize the drama of the life and death impulses that drive the characters on to their fates and put more in its proper secondary place, as a frame, the story of the New England family.

A Dramatist's Notebook[3] (1933)

I advocate masks for stage crowds, mobs—wherever a sense of impersonal, collective mob psychology is wanted. This was one reason for such an extensive use of them in *Lazarus Laughed.* In masking the crowds in that play, I was visualizing an effect that, intensified by dramatic lighting, would give an audience visually the sense of the Crowd, not as a random collection of individuals, but as a collective whole, an entity. When the Crowd speaks, I

[3] Eugene O'Neill, "A Dramatist's Notebook," *The American Spectator,* January, 1933, p. 2.

wanted an audience to hear the voice of Crowd mind,
Crowd emotion, as one voice of a body composed of, but
quite distinct from, its parts.

And, for more practical reasons, I wanted to preserve
the different crowds of another time and country from the
blighting illusion-shattering recognitions by an audience
of the supers on the stage. Have you ever seen a production of *Julius Caesar?* Did the Roman mob ever suggest to
you anything more Roman than a gum-chewing Coney
Island Mardi Gras or, in the case of a special all-star
revival, a gathering of familiar-faced modern actors
masquerading uncomfortably in togas? But with masks—
and the proper intensive lighting—you would have been
freed from these recognitions; you would have been able
to imagine a Roman mob; you would not even have recognized the Third Avenue and Brooklyn accents among the
supers, so effectively does a mask change the quality of a
voice.

It was interesting to watch, in the final rehearsals of
The Great God Brown, how after using their masks for
a time the actors and actresses reacted to the demand
made by the masks that their bodies become alive and
expressive and participate in the drama. Usually it is only
the actors' faces that participate. Their bodies remain bored
spectators that have been dragged off to the theatre when
they would have much preferred a quiet evening in the
upholstered chair at home.

Meaning no carping disrespect to our actors. I have
been exceedingly lucky in having had some exceptionally
fine acting in the principal roles in my plays, for which I am
exceedingly grateful. Also some damned poor acting. But
let that pass. Most of the poor acting occurred in the
poor plays, and there I hold only myself responsible. In
the main, wherever a part challenged the actors' or actresses' greatest possibilities, they have reacted to the challenge with a splendid creative energy and skill. Especially,
and this is the point I want to make now, where the play
took them away from the strictly realistic parts they were
accustomed to playing. They always welcomed any opportunity that gave them new scope for their talents. So
when I argue here for a non-realistic imaginative theatre
I am hoping, not only for added scope for playwright
and director and scenic designer, but also for a chance for
the actor to develop his art beyond the narrow range to

which our present theatre condemns it. Most important of all, from the standpoint of future American culture, I am hoping for added imaginative scope for the audience, a chance for a public I know is growing yearly more numerous and more hungry in its spiritual need to participate in imaginative interpretations of life rather than merely identify itself with faithful surface resemblances of living.

I harp on the word "imaginative" — and with intention! But what do I mean by an "imaginative" theatre — (where I hope for it, for example, in the subtitle of *Lazarus Laughed*: A Play for an Imaginative Theatre)? I mean the one true theatre, the age-old theatre, the theatre of the Greeks and Elizabethans, a theatre that could dare to boast — without committing a farcical sacrilege — that it is a legitimate descendant of the first theatre that sprang, by virtue of man's imaginative interpretation of life, out of his worship of Dionysus. I mean a theatre returned to its highest and sole significant function as a Temple where the religion of a poetical interpretation and symbolical celebration of life is communicated to human beings, starved in spirit by their soul-stifling daily struggle to exist as masks among the masks of living!

But I anticipate the actors' objection to masks: that they would extinguish their personalities and deprive them of their greatest asset in conveying emotion by facial expression. I claim, however, that masks would give them the opportunity for a totally new kind of acting, that they would learn many undeveloped possibilities of their art if they appeared, even if only for a season or two, in masked roles. After all, masks did not extinguish the Greek actor, nor have they kept the acting of the East from being an art.

BERTOLT BRECHT
(1898-1956)

A Short Organum for the Theatre[1] (1948)

PROLOGUE

THE FOLLOWING sets out to define an aesthetic drawn
from a particular kind of theatrical performance which
has been worked out in practice over the past few decades.
In the theoretical statements, excursions, technical indications occasionally published in the form of notes to the
writer's plays, aesthetics have only been touched on
casually and with comparative lack of interest. There you
saw a particular species of theatre extending or contracting
its social function, perfecting or sifting its artistic methods,
and establishing or maintaining its aesthetics—if the question arose—by rejecting or converting to its own use the
dominant conventions of morality or taste according to its
tactical needs. This theatre justified its tendency to draw
social conclusions by pointing to the social conclusions in
universally accepted works of art, which only fail to
strike the eye because they were the accepted conclusions.
As for the products of our own time, it held that their
lack of any worthwhile content was a sign of decadence; it
accused these entertainment emporiums of having degen-
erated into a branch of the bourgeois narcotics traffic.
The stage's inaccurate representations of our social life,
including those classed as so-called Naturalism, led it
to call for scientifically exact representations; the taste-
less rehashing of empty visual or spiritual palliatives
for the noble logic of the multiplication table. The cult
of beauty, conducted with hostility toward learning
and contempt for the useful, was dismissed by it as
itself contemptible, especially as nothing beautiful re-

[1] Bertolt Brecht, "Kleines Organon für das Theater," Ver-
suche, 12 (Frankfurt-am-Main: Suhrkamp Verlag). Copyright
1953 by Suhrkamp Verlag, Berlin. Translated by John Willett,
and edited by Eric Bentley. Reprinted by permission of Suhrkamp Verlag and John Willett.

sulted. The battle was for a theatre fit for the scientific age, and where its planners found it too hard to borrow or steal from the armory of aesthetic concepts enough weapons to defend themselves against the aesthetes of the press, they simply threatened "to transform the means of enjoyment into an instrument of instruction, and to convert certain amusement establishments into organs of mass communication" (Notes to the opera *Mahagonny*[2]); i.e., to emigrate from the realm of the merely enjoyable. Aesthetics, that heirloom of a now depraved and parasitic class, was in such a lamentable state that a *Theater* would certainly have gained in reputation and in elbow room if it had rechristened itself *Thaeter* [sic]. And yet what we achieved in the way of theatre for a scientific age was not science but theatre, and the accumulated innovations worked out during the Nazi period and the war—when practical demonstration was impossible—compel some attempt to set this species of theatre in its aesthetic background, or anyhow to sketch for it the outlines of a conceivable aesthetic. It would be an impossibly laborious business to explain the theory of theatrical Alienation[3] except within an aesthetic framework.

Today one could go so far as to compile an aesthetics of the exact sciences. Galileo spoke of the elegance of certain formulae and the point of an experiment; Einstein suggests that the sense of beauty has a part to play in the making of scientific discoveries; while the atomic physicist Robert Oppenheimer praises the scientific attitude, which

[2] A translation of *Mahagonny* is to be found in the *Mahagonny* record album, Columbia Records, New York, 1958. A translation of the Notes by John Willett is published in *The Score* (London: July, 1958). Excerpts appear in the Columbia album and in *The Playwright as Thinker* (New York: 1946) (E. B.).

[3] "Alienation" has become, in America at least, the standard translation of *Verfremdung*. It is not a perfect solution of the problem, as the English word has other meanings in translations of, for example, both Marx and Freud. "Estrangement," however, is probably even more confusing and would be translated into German as *Entfremdung*—even though the latter word has often been translated into English as Alienation! There *is* no perfect solution. The word Effect (in Alienation Effect) also gives trouble. As Mr. Willett says (*The Theatre of Bertolt Brecht*, p. 179): ". . . *Effekt* corresponded to our own stage use of the word *effects*: a *means* by which an effect of estrangement could be got" (E. B.).

"has its own kind of beauty and seems to suit mankind's position on earth."[4]

So let us cause general dismay by revoking our decision to emigrate from the realm of the merely enjoyable, and even more general dismay by announcing our decision to take up lodging there. Let us treat the theatre as a place of entertainment, as is proper in an aesthetic discussion, and try to discover what kind of entertainment suits us best.

(1)

"Theatre" consists in this: in making live representations of reported or invented happenings between human beings, and doing so with a view to entertainment. At any rate that is what we shall mean when we speak of theatre, whether old or new.

(2)

To extend this definition we might add happenings between humans and gods, but as we are only seeking to establish bare essentials we can set such matters aside. Even if we did accept such an extension we should still have to say that the "theatre" setup's broadest function was to give pleasure. Here is the noblest function that we have found for "theatre."

(3)

From the first it has been the theatre's business to entertain people, as it also has of all the other arts. It is this business which always gives it its particular dignity; it needs no other passport than fun, but this it has got to have. We should not in any way be giving it a higher status if we were to turn it, e.g., into a purveyor of morality; it would on the contrary run the risk of becoming debased, and this would occur just as soon as it failed to make its moral lesson enjoyable, and enjoyable to the senses at that—a principle, admittedly, by which morality can only gain. Not even instruction can be demanded of it; at any rate, no more utilitarian lesson than how to

[4] Dr. Oppenheimer's secretary reported to me her inability to locate the source of this remark, here translated from the German (E. B.).

move pleasurably, whether in the physical or in the spiritual sphere. The theatre must in short remain something entirely superfluous, though this also means that it is the superfluous for which we live. Nothing needs less justification than pleasures.

(4)

Thus what the ancients, following Aristotle, demanded of tragedy is nothing higher or lower than that it should entertain people. Theatre may be said to be derived from ritual, but that is only to say that it becomes theatre once the two have separated; what it brought over from the mysteries was not its former ritual function, but purely and simply the pleasure which accompanied this. And the catharsis of which Aristotle writes—cleansing by fear and pity, or from fear and pity—is a purification which is performed not only in a pleasurable way, but precisely for the purpose of pleasure. To ask or to accept more of the theatre is to set one's own mark too low.

(5)

Even when people speak of higher and lower degrees of pleasure, art stares impassively back at them; for it wishes to fly high and low and to be left in peace, so long as it can give pleasure to people.

(6)

Yet there are weaker (simple) and stronger (complex) pleasures which the theatre can create. The last-named, which are what we are dealing with in great drama, attain their climaxes rather like cohabitation does in love; they are more intricate, richer in communication, more contradictory and more productive of results.

(7)

And different periods' pleasures varied naturally according to the system under which people lived in society at the time. The Greek demos[5] ruled by tyrants had to be enter-

---

[5] Literally "the demos of the Greek circus" (J. W.).

tained differently from the feudal court of Louis XIV.
The theatre was required to deliver different representations of human social life: not just representations of a
different life, but also representations of a different sort.

(8)

According to the sort of entertainment which was
possible and necessary under the given conditions of
human social life the characters had to be given varying proportions, the situations to be constructed according to varying points of view. One has to tell a story in
quite different ways if these particular Greeks are to be
able to amuse themselves with the inevitability of divine
laws, where ignorance never mitigates the punishment; these
French with the graceful self-discipline demanded of the
great ones of this earth by a courtly code of duty; the
Englishmen of the Elizabethan age with the self-awareness
of the new individual personality, which was then uncon-
trollably bursting out.

(9)

And we have always to remember that the pleasure
given by representations of such different sorts hardly
ever depended on the representation's likeness to the thing
portrayed. Incorrectness, or considerable improbability
even, was hardly or not at all disturbing, so long as the
incorrectness had a certain consistency and the improbability remained of a constant kind. All that mattered was
the illusion of compelling momentum in the story told, and
this was created by all sorts of poetic and theatrical
means. Even today we are happy to overlook such in-
accuracies if we can get something out of the spiritual
purifications of Sophocles or the sacrificial acts of Racine
or the unbridled frenzies of Shakespeare, by trying to
grasp the immense or splendid emotions of the principal
characters concerned.

(10)

For of all the many sorts of representation of happenings between humans which the theatre has made since
ancient times, and which have given entertainment despite
their incorrectness and improbability, there are even

today an astonishing number that also give entertainment to us.

(11)

In establishing the extent to which we can be satisfied by representations from so many different periods —something that must have been impossible to the children of those vigorous periods themselves—are we not at the same time creating the suspicion that we have failed to discover the special pleasures, the proper entertainment of our own time?

(12)

Again, our enjoyment of the theatre must have become weaker than that of the ancients, even if our way of living in society is still sufficiently like theirs for it to be felt at all. We grasp the old works by a comparatively new method—empathy—on which they rely little. Thus the greater part of our enjoyment is drawn from other sources than those which our predecessors were able to exploit so fully. We are left safely dependent on beauty of language, on elegance of structure, on passages which stimulate our own private imaginations; in short, on the incidentals of the old works. These are precisely the poetical and theatrical means which hide the imprecisions of the story. Our theatres no longer have either the capacity or the wish to tell these stories, even the relatively recent ones of the great Shakespeare, at all clearly; i.e., to make the connection of events credible. And according to Aristotle—and we agree there—narrative is the soul of drama. We are more and more disturbed to see how crudely and carelessly human social life is represented, and that not only in old works but also in contemporary ones constructed according to the old recipes. Our whole way of appreciation is tending to get out of date.

(13)

It is the inaccurate way in which happenings between human beings are represented that restricts our pleasure in the theatre. The reason: we and our forebears have a different relationship to what is being shown.

(14)

For when we look about us for an entertainment whose impact is immediate, for a comprehensive and penetrating pleasure such as our theatre could give us by representations of human social life, we have to think of ourselves as children of a scientific age. Our life as human beings in society—i.e., our life—is determined by the sciences to a quite new extent.

(15)

A few hundred years ago a handful of people, working in different countries but in correspondence with one another, performed certain experiments by which they hoped to wring from Nature her secrets. Members of a class of craftsmen in the already powerful cities, they transmitted their discoveries to people who made practical use of them, without expecting more from the new sciences than personal profit for themselves. Crafts which had progressed by methods virtually unchanged during a thousand years now developed hugely; in many places, which became linked by competition, they gathered from all directions great masses of men, and these, adopting new forms of organization, started producing on a giant scale. Soon mankind was showing powers whose extent it would till that time scarcely have dared to dream of.

(16)

It was as if mankind now for the first time began a conscious and co-ordinated effort to make the planet that was its home fit to live on. Many of the earth's components, such as coal, water, oil, now became treasures. Steam was made to shift vehicles; a few small sparks and the twitching of frogs' legs revealed a natural force which produced light, carried sounds across continents, etc. In all directions man looked about himself with a new vision, to see how he could adapt to his convenience familiar but as yet unexploited objects. His surroundings changed increasingly from decade to decade, then from year to year, then almost from day to day. I who am writing this write it on a machine which at the time of my birth was unknown. I travel in the new vehicles with a rapidity that my grandfather could not imagine;

in those days nothing moved so fast. And I rise in the air, a thing that my father was unable to do. With my father I already spoke across the width of a continent, but it was together with my son that I first saw the motion pictures of the explosion at Hiroshima.

(17)

The new sciences may have made possible this vast alteration and all-important alterability of our surroundings, yet it cannot be said that their spirit determines everything that we do. The reason why the new way of thinking and feeling has not yet penetrated the great mass of men is that the sciences, for all their success in exploiting and dominating nature, have been stopped by the class which they brought to power—the bourgeoisie —from operating in another field where darkness still reigns, namely that of the relations which people have to one another during the exploiting and dominating process. This business, on which all alike depended, was performed without the new intellectual methods that made it possible, ever illuminating the mutual relationships of the people who carried it out. The new approach to nature was not applied to society.

(18)

In the event people's mutual relations have become harder to disentangle than ever before. The gigantic joint undertaking on which they are engaged seems more and more to split them into two groups; increases in production lead to increases in misery; only a minority gain from the exploitation of nature, and they do so only because they also exploit men. What might be progress for all then becomes advancement for a few, and an ever-increasing part of the productive process gets applied to creating means of destruction for mighty wars. During these wars the mothers of every nation, with their children pressed to them, scan the skies in horror for the deadly inventions of science.

(19)

The same attitude as men once showed in face of unpredictable natural catastrophes they now adopt toward

their own undertakings. The bourgeois class, which owes
to science an advancement that it was able, by insuring
that it alone enjoyed the fruits, to convert into domi-
nation, knows very well that its rule would come to an
end if the scientific eye were turned on its own undertakings. And so that new science which was founded about
a hundred years ago and deals with the character of
human society was born in the struggle between rulers
and ruled. Since then a certain scientific spirit has developed at the bottom, among the new class of workers
whose natural element is large-scale production; from
down there the great catastrophes are seen to be undertakings by the rulers.

(20)

But science and art meet on this ground, that both
are there to make men's life easier, the one setting out
to maintain, the other to entertain us. In the age to come
art will create entertainment from that new productivity
which can so greatly improve our maintenance and in itself,
if only it is left unshackled, may prove to be the greatest
pleasure of them all.

(21)

If we want now to surrender ourselves to this great
passion for producing, what ought our representations of
human social life to look like? Which is that productive
attitude in face of nature and of society which we children
of a scientific age would like to take up pleasurably in
our theatre?

(22)

The attitude is a critical one. Faced with a river, it
consists in regulating the river; faced with a fruit tree, in
spraying the fruit tree; faced with movement, in construct-
ing vehicles and airplanes; faced with society, in turning
society upside down. Our representations of human social
life are designed for river dwellers, fruit farmers, build-
ers of vehicles, and upturners of society, whom we invite
into our theatres and beg not to forget their cheerful
occupations while we hand the world over to their minds
and hearts, for them to change as they think fit.

(23)

The theatre can only adopt such a free attitude if it lets itself be carried along by the strongest currents in its society, and associates itself with those who are necessarily most impatient to carry out great alterations there. The bare wish, if nothing else, to evolve an art fit for the times must drive our theatre of the scientific age straight out into the suburbs, where it can stand as it were wide open, at the disposal of those who live hard and produce much, so that they may be fruitfully entertained there with their great problems. They may find it hard to pay for our art, and immediately to grasp the new method of entertainment, and we shall have to learn in many respects what they need and how they need it; but we can be sure of their interest. For these men who seem so far apart from natural science are only apart from it because they are being forcibly kept apart; before they can get their hands on it they have first to develop and put into effect a new science of society; so that these are the true children of the scientific age, who alone can get the theatre moving if it is to move at all. A theatre which makes productivity its main source of entertainment has also to take it for its theme, with greater keenness than ever now that man is everywhere hampered by men from self-production; i.e., from maintaining himself, from entertaining and being entertained. The theatre has to become geared into reality if it is to be in a position to turn out effective representations of reality, and to be allowed to do so.

(24)

But this makes it simpler for the theatre to edge as close as possible to the apparatus of education and mass communication. For although we cannot bother it with the raw material of knowledge in all its variety, which would stop it from being enjoyable, it is still free to find enjoyment in teaching and inquiring. It constructs its workable representations of society, which are then in a position to influence society, wholly and entirely as a game. For those who are building society it sets out society's experiences, past and present alike, in such a manner that the audience can "appreciate" the feelings, insights, and impulses which are distilled by the wisest, most active, and most passionate among us from the events of the day or the century. They must be entertained with the wisdom that comes from the solution of problems, with the anger that is a practical expression of sympathy with the underdog, with the respect due to those who respect humanity, or rather whatever is kind to humanity; in short, with whatever delights those who are producing something.

(25)

This also means that the theatre can let its spectators enjoy the particular ethic of their age, which springs from productivity. A theatre which converts the critical approach—i.e., our great productive method—into pleasure finds nothing in the ethical field which it must do and a great deal that it can. Even the wholly antisocial can be a source of enjoyment to society so long as it is presented forcefully and on the grand scale. It then often proves to have considerable powers of understanding and other unusually valuable capacities, applied admittedly to a destructive end. Even the bursting flood of a vast catastrophe can be appreciated in all its majesty by society, if society knows how to master it. Then we make it our own.

(26)

For such an operation as this we can hardly accept the theatre as we see it before us. Let us go into one of these houses and observe the effect which it has on the spectators. Looking about us, we see somewhat motionless figures in a peculiar condition: they seem strenuously to be tensing all their muscles, except where these are flabby and exhausted. They scarcely communicate with each other; their relations are those of a lot of sleepers, though of such as dream restlessly because, as is popularly said of those who have nightmares, they are lying on their backs. True, their eyes are open, but they stare rather than see, just as they listen rather than hear. They look at the stage as if in a trance, an expression which comes from the Middle Ages, the days of witches and priests. Seeing and hearing are activities, and can be pleasant ones, but these people seem relieved of activity and like men to whom something is being done. This detached state, where they seem to be given over to vague but profound sensations, grows deeper the better the work of the actors, and so we, as we do not approve of this situation, should like them to be as bad as possible.

(27)

As for the world portrayed there, the world from which slices are cut in order to produce these moods and movements of the emotions, its appearance is such, produced from such slight and wretched stuff as a few pieces of cardboard, a little miming, a bit of text, that one has to admire the theatre folk who, with so feeble a reflection of the real world, can move the feelings of their audience so much more strongly than does the world itself.

(28)

In any case we should excuse these theatre folk, for the pleasures which they sell for money and fame could not be induced by an exacter representation of the world, nor could their inexact renderings be presented in a less magical way. Their capacity to represent people can be seen at work in various instances; it is especially the rogues and the minor figures who reveal their knowledge of humanity and differ one from the other, but the central figures have to be kept general, so that it is easier for the onlooker to identify himself with them, and at all costs each trait of character must be drawn from the narrow field within which everyone can say at once: that is how it is. For the spectator wants to be put in possession of quite definite sensations, just as a child does when it climbs onto one of the horses on a roundabout: the sensation of pride that it can ride, and has a horse; the pleasure of being carried, and whirled past other children; the adventurous daydreams in which it pursues others or is pursued, etc. In leading the child to experience all this the degree to which its wooden seat resembles a horse counts little, nor does it matter that the ride is confined to a small circle. The one important point for the spectators in these houses is that they should be able to swap a contradictory world for a consistent one,

one that they scarcely know for one of which they can dream.

(29)

This is the sort of theatre which we face in our operations, and so far it has been fully able to transmute our optimistic friends, whom we have called the children of the scientific era, into a cowed, credulous, hypnotized mass.

(30)

True, for about half a century they have been able to see rather more faithful representations of human social life, as well as individual figures who were in revolt against certain social evils or even against the structure of society as a whole. They felt interested enough to put up with a temporary and exceptional restriction of language, plot, and spiritual scope, for the fresh wind of the scientific spirit nearly withered the charms to which they had grown used. The sacrifice was not especially worthwhile. The greater subtlety of the representations subtracted from one pleasure without satisfying another. The field of human relationships came within our view, but not within our grasp. Our feelings, having been aroused in the old (magic) way, were bound themselves to remain unaltered.

(31)

For always and everywhere theatres were the amusement centers of a class which restricted the scientific spirit to the natural field, not daring to let it loose on the field of human relationships. The tiny proletarian section of the public, reinforced to a negligible and uncertain extent by renegade intellectuals, likewise still needed the old kind of entertainment as a relief from its predetermined way of life.

(32)

So let us march ahead! Away with all obstacles! Since we seem to have landed in a battle, let us fight! Have we not seen how disbelief can move mountains? Is it not enough that we should have found that something is being kept from us? Before one thing and another there hangs a curtain; let us draw it up!

(33)

The theatre as we know it shows the structure of society (represented on the stage) as incapable of being influenced by society (in the auditorium). Oedipus, who offended against certain principles underlying the society of his time, is executed: the gods see to that; they are beyond criticism. Shakespeare's great solitary figures, bearing on their breast the star of their fate, carry through with irresistible force their futile and deadly outbursts; they prepare their own downfall; life, not death, becomes obscene as they collapse; the catastrophe is beyond criticism. Human sacrifices all round! Barbaric delights! We know that the barbarians have their art. Let us create another.

(34)

How much longer are our souls, leaving our "mere" bodies under cover of the darkness, to plunge into those dreamlike figures up on the stage, there to take part in the crescendos and climaxes which "normal" life denies us? What kind of release is it at the end of all these plays (which is a happy end only for the conventions of the period—suitable measures, the restoration of order—), when we experience the dreamlike executioner's ax which cuts short such crescendos as so many excesses? We slink into *Oedipus*; for taboos still exist and ignorance is no excuse before the law. Into *Othello*; for jealousy still causes us trouble and everything depends on possession. Into *Wallenstein*; for we need to be free for the competitive struggle and to observe the rules, or it would peter out. This deadweight of old habits is also needed for plays like *Ghosts* and *The Weavers*, although there the social structure, in the shape of a "setting," presents itself as more open to question. The feelings, insights, and impulses of the chief characters are forced on us, and so we learn nothing more about society than the setting can give.

(35)

We need a type of theatre which not only releases the feelings, insights, and impulses possible within the partic-

ular historical field of human relations in which the action
takes place, but employs and encourages those thoughts
and feelings which help transform the field itself.

(36)

This field has to be defined in historically relative
terms. In other words we must drop our habit of taking
the different social structures of past periods, then strip-
ping them of everything that makes them different; until
they all look more or less like our own, which then acquires
a certain air of having been there all along, in other words
of permanence pure and simple. Instead we must leave
them their distinguishing marks and keep their imperma-
nence always before our eyes, so that our own period can
be realized to be impermanent too. (It is of course futile
to make use of gaudy coloring and folklore for this, such
as our theatres apply precisely in order to emphasize the
similarities in human behavior at different times. We shall
indicate the theatrical methods below.)

(37)

If we insure that our characters on the stage are moved
by social impulses and that these differ according to the
period, then we make it harder for our spectator to identify himself with them. He cannot just feel: that's how I
would act, but at most can say: if I had lived under those
circumstances. And if we play works dealing with our own
time as though they too were historical, then perhaps the
circumstances under which he himself acts will strike
him as equally odd; and this is where the critical attitude
begins.

(38)

The "historical conditions" must of course not be imagined (nor will they be so constructed) as mysterious
Powers (in the background); on the contrary, they are
created and maintained by men (and will in due course
be altered by them). It is the actions taking place before
us that allow us to see what they are.

(39)

If a character responds in a manner historically in
keeping with his period, and would respond otherwise in

other periods, does that not mean that he is simply
"Everyman"? Undoubtedly a man will respond differently
according to his circumstances and his class; if he were
living at another time, or in his youth, or on the darker
side of life, he would infallibly give a different response,
though one still determined by the same factors and
like anyone else's response in that position at that time.
So should we not ask if there are further differences
too? Where is the man himself, the living, unmistakable
man, who is not quite identical with those identified with
him? It is clear that his stage image must bring him to
light, and that this particular contradiction is recreated in
the image. The image that gives historical definition will
retain something of the rough sketching which indicates
traces of other movements and features all around the
fully worked-out figure. Or imagine a man standing in a
valley and making a speech in which he occasionally
switches his views or simply utters sentences which contra-
dict one another, so that the accompanying echo as it were
confronts them.

(40)

Such images certainly demand a way of acting which
will leave the spectator's intellect free and highly mobile.
He has again and again to make what one might call
hypothetical adjustments to our structure, by mentally
switching off the motive forces of our society or by substituting others for them; a process which leads real conduct to acquire an element of "unnaturalness," thus allowing the real motive forces to be shorn of their naturalness and to become capable of manipulation.

(41)

It is the same as when an irrigation expert looks at a
river together with its former bed and the various hypothetical courses which it might have followed if there had
been a different tilt to the plateau or a different volume
of water. And while he in his mind is looking at a new
river, the socialist in his is hearing new kinds of talk from
the laborers who work by it. Similarly in the theatre, the
spectator should find the incidents set among such laborers likewise accompanied by echoes and by traces of
sketching.

(42)

The kind of acting which was tried out at the Schiff-
bauerdamm-Theater in Berlin between the first and second
World Wars, with the object of producing such images,
is based on a technique of creating detachment, known
as the Alienation Effect. A representation that creates
detachment is one which allows us to recognize its subject, but at the same time makes it seem unfamiliar. The
classical and medieval theatre defamiliarized its characters by making them wear human or animal masks; the
Asiatic theatre even today uses musical and pantomimic
A Effects. Such devices were certainly a barrier to empathy (*Einfühlung*), and yet this technique owed more,
not less, to hypnotic suggestion than do those by which
empathy is achieved. The social aims of these old devices
were entirely different from our own.

(43)

The old A Effects quite remove the object represented
from the spectator's grasp, turning it into something that
cannot be altered. The new are not odd in themselves,
though the unscientific eye stamps anything strange as
odd. The new detachment is only designed to free socially
conditioned phenomena from that stamp of familiarity
which protects them against our grasp today.

(44)

For it seems impossible to alter what has long not
been altered. We are always coming on things that are
too obvious for us to bother to understand them. What
men experience among themselves they think of as "the"
human experience. A child, living in a world of old men,
learns how things work there. He knows the run of things
before he can walk. If anyone is bold enough to want
something further, he only wants to have it as an exception. Even if he realizes that the arrangements made for
him by "Providence" are only what has been provided by
society he is bound to see society, that vast collection of
beings like himself, as a whole that is greater than the sum
of its parts, and therefore not in any way to be influenced.
Moreover, he is accustomed to things that cannot be

influenced; and who mistrusts what he is used to? To transform himself from general passive acceptance to a corresponding state of suspicious inquiry he needs to develop that detached eye with which the great Galileo observed a swinging chandelier. He was amazed by this pendulum motion, as if he had not expected it and could not understand its occurring, and this enabled him to come on the rules by which it was governed. Here is the outlook, disconcerting but fruitful, which the theatre must provoke with its representations of human social life. It must amaze its public, and it achieves this by a technique of making the familiar seem strange.

(45)

This technique allows the theatre to make use in its representations of the new social scientific method known as dialectical materialism. In order to unearth society's laws of motion this method treats social situations as processes, and traces out all their inconsistencies. It regards nothing as existing except in so far as it changes; in other words, is in disharmony with itself. This also goes for those human feelings, opinions, and attitudes through which at any time the form of human social life finds its expression.

(46)

Our own period, which is transforming nature in so many and different ways, takes pleasure in understanding things so that we can intervene. There is a great deal to man, we say; so a great deal can be made out of him. He does not have to stay the way he is now, nor does he have to be seen only as he is now, but also as he might become. We must not start with him; we must start on him. This means, however, that I must not simply set myself in his place, but must set myself facing him, to represent us all. That is why the theatre must make what it shows seem strange.

(47)

In order to produce A Effects the actor has to discard whatever means he has learned of persuading the audience to identify itself with the characters which he plays. Aiming not to put his audience into a trance, he must not go into a trance himself. His muscles must remain loose, for a turn of the head, e.g., with tautened neck muscles, will "magically" lead the spectators' eyes and even their heads to turn with it, and this can only detract from any speculation or reaction which the gesture may bring about. His way of speaking has to be free from ecclesiastical singsong and from all those cadences which lull the spectator so that the sense gets lost. Even when he plays a man possessed he must not seem to be possessed himself, for how can the spectator discover what possesses the character if he does?

(48)

At no moment must he go so far as to be wholly transformed into the character played. The verdict: "He didn't act Lear, he was Lear" would be an annihilating blow to him. He has just to show the character, or rather he has to do more than just get into it; this does not mean that if he is playing passionate parts he must himself remain cold. It is only that his feelings must not at bottom be those of the character, so that the audience's may not at bottom be those of the character either. The audience must have complete freedom here.

(49)

This principle—that the actor appears on the stage in a double role, as Laughton and as Galileo; that the showman Laughton does not disappear in the Galileo whom he is showing; from which this way of acting gets its name of "epic"—comes to mean simply that the tangible, matter-of-fact process is no longer hidden behind a veil; that Laughton is actually there, standing on the stage and showing us what he imagines Galileo to have been. Of course the audience would not forget Laughton if he attempted the full change of personality, in that they would admire him for it; but they would in that case miss his own opinions and sensations, which would have been completely swallowed up by the character. He would have taken its opinions and sensations and made them his own, so that a single homogeneous pattern would emerge, which he would then make ours. In order to prevent this abuse the actor must furthermore put some artistry into the act of showing. An illustration may help: we find a gesture which expresses one half of his attitude, that of showing,

if we make him smoke a cigar and then imagine him lay-
ing it down now and again in order to show us some further
characteristic attitude of the figure in the play. If we then
subtract all element of hurry from the image, and do
not read slackness into its refusal to be taut, we shall have
an actor who is fully capable of leaving us to our thoughts,
or to his own.

(50)

There needs to be yet a further change in the actor's
communication of these images, and it too makes the
process more "matter-of-fact." Just as the actor no longer
has to persuade the audience that it is the author's character and not he himself who is standing on the stage, so
also he need not pretend that the events taking place on
the stage have never been rehearsed, and are now hap-
pening for the first and only time. Schiller's distinction is
no longer valid: that the rhapsodist has to treat his material as wholly in the past; the mime his as wholly here and
now.[6] It should be apparent all through his performance
that "even at the start and in the middle he knows how
it ends" and he must "thus maintain a calm independence
throughout." He narrates the story of his character by
vivid portrayal, always knowing more than it does and
treating its "now" and "here" not as a pretense made
possible by the rules of the game, but as something to be
distinguished from yesterday and some other place, so as
to make visible the knotting together of the events.

(51)

This matters particularly in the portrayal of large-scale
events or ones where the outside world is abruptly changed,
as in wars and revolutions. The spectator can then have
the whole situation and the whole course of events set before him. He can, for instance, hear a woman speaking
and imagine her speaking differently, let us say in a few
weeks' time, or other women speaking differently at that
moment but in another place. This would be feasible if
the actress were to play as though the woman had lived
through the entire period and were now, out of her memory
and her knowledge of what happened next, recalling those

[6] Letter to Goethe, December 26, 1797 (B. B.).

utterances of hers which were important at the time; for
what is important here is what became important. To
make an individual seem unfamiliar in this way, as being
"this particular individual" and "this particular individual
at this particular moment" is only possible if there are
no illusions that the player is identical with the character,
or the performance with the actual event.

(52)

We shall find that this has meant scrapping yet another
illusion: that everybody behaves like the character concerned. "I am doing this" has become "I did this," and
now "he did this" has got to become "he did this, when
he might have done something else." It is an oversimpli-
fication if we make the actions fit the character and the
character fit the actions; the inconsistencies which are to
be found in the actions and characters of real people cannot be shown like that. The laws of motion of a society are
not to be demonstrated by "perfect examples," for "im-
perfection" (inconsistency) is an essential part both of
motion and of the thing moved. It is only necessary—but
absolutely necessary—that there should be something approaching experimental conditions: i.e., that a counter-
experiment should now and then be conceivable. In short,
this is a way of treating society as though all its actions
were performed as experiments.

(53)

Even if empathy, or self-identification with the character, can be usefully indulged in at rehearsals (something to be avoided in a performance), it has to be treated
as just one of a number of methods of observation. It
can help when rehearsing, for even though the contemporary theatre has applied it in an indiscriminate way it
has none the less led to subtle delineation of personality.
But it is the crudest form of empathy when the actor
simply asks: what should I be like if this or that were to
happen to me? what would it look like if I were to say this
and do that?—instead of asking: have I ever heard somebody saying this and doing that? in order to piece together all sorts of elements with which to construct a new

character such as would allow the story to have taken place
—and a good deal else. The coherence of the character
is in fact shown by the way in which its individual qualities
conflict with one another.

(54)

Observation is a major part of acting. The actor observes his fellow-men with all his nerves and muscles, in an
act of imitation which is at the same time a process of
the mind. For pure imitation would only bring out what
had been observed; and this is not enough, because the
original says what it has to say with too subdued a voice.
To achieve a character rather than a caricature, the actor
looks at people as though they were playing him their
actions, in other words as though they were advising him
to give their actions careful consideration.

(55)

Without opinions and objectives one can represent
nothing at all. Without knowledge one can show nothing;
how could one know what would be worth knowing? Unless the actor is satisfied to be a parrot or a monkey he
must master our period's knowledge of human social life
by himself joining in the war of the classes. Some people
may feel this to be degrading, because they rank art, once
the financial side has been settled, among the Highest
Things; but mankind's highest decisions are in fact fought
out on earth, not in the heavens; in the "external" world,
not inside people's heads. Nobody can stand above the
warring classes, for nobody can stand above the human
race. Society cannot share a common communication system so long as it is split into warring classes. For art,
to be "unpolitical" means only that it should ally itself
with the ruling group.

(56)

So the choice of viewpoint is also a major element of
the actor's art, and it has to be decided outside the theatre.
Like the transformation of nature, that of society is a
liberating act; and it is the joys of liberation which the
theatre of a scientific age has got to convey.

(57)

Let us go on to examine how, for instance, this view-point must affect the actor's reading of his part. It becomes important that he should not "catch on" too quickly. Even if he straightway establishes the most natural cadences for his part, the least awkward way of speaking it, he still cannot regard its actual pronouncement as being ideally natural, but must think twice and take his own general opinions into account, then consider various other conceivable pronouncements; in short, take up the attitude of a man who just wonders. This is not only to prevent him from "fixing" a particular character too soon, so that it has to be stuffed out with afterthoughts because he has not waited to register all the other pronouncements, and especially those of the other characters; but also and principally in order to build into the character that element of "Not—But" on which so much depends if society, in the shape of the audience, is to be able to look at what takes place in such a way as to be able to affect it. Each actor, moreover, instead of concentrating on what suits him and calling it "human nature," must go above all for what does not suit him, is not his speciality. And along with his part he must commit to memory his first reactions, reserves, criticisms, shocks, so that they are not destroyed by being "swallowed up" in the final version but are preserved and perceptible; for character and all must not grow on the audience so much as strike it.

(58)

And the learning process must be co-ordinated so that the actor learns as the other actors are learning and develops his character as they are developing theirs. For the smallest social unit is not the single person but two people. In life too we develop one another.

(59)

Here we can learn something from our own theatre's deplorable habit of letting the dominant actor, the star, "come to the front" by getting all the other actors to work for him: he makes his character terrible or wise by forcing his partners to make theirs terrified or attentive.

Even if only to secure this advantage for all, and thus to help the story, the actors should sometimes swap roles with their partners during rehearsal, so that the characters can get what they need from one another. But it is also good for the actors when they see their characters copied or portrayed in another form. If the part is played by somebody of the opposite sex, the sex of the character will be more clearly brought out; if it is played by a comedian, whether comically or tragically, it will gain fresh aspects. By helping to develop the parts that correspond to his own, or at any rate standing in for their players, the actor strengthens the all-decisive social standpoint from which he has to present his character. The master is only the sort of master his servant lets him be, and so on.

(60)

A mass of operations to develop the character are carried out when it is introduced among the other characters of the play; and the actor will have to memorize what he himself has anticipated in this connection from his reading of the text. But now he finds out much more about himself from the treatment which he gets at the hands of the characters in the play.

(61)

The realm of attitudes adopted by the characters toward one another is what we call the realm of *Gestus*.[7] Physical attitude, tone of voice, and facial expression are all determined by a social *Gestus:* the characters are cursing, flattering, instructing one another, and so on. The attitudes which people adopt toward one another include even those attitudes which would appear to be quite private, such as the utterances of physical pain in an illness, or of religious faith. These expressions of a *Gestus* are usually highly complicated and self-contradictory, so

[7] This word has been left in German because its most natural English equivalent—the word Gesture—is far more misleading than even Alienation (as a translation of *Verfremdung*). I quote Mr. Willett (*The Theatre of Bertolt Brecht*, p. 175): ". . . there is no single word by which *Gestus* can be translated. It is at once gesture and gist, attitude and point: one aspect of the relation between two people, studied singly, cut to essentials and physically or verbally expressed . . ." (E. B.).

that they cannot be rendered by any single word, and the
actor must take care that in giving his image the necessary emphasis he does not lose anything but emphasizes
the entire complex.

(62)

The actor masters his character by paying critical attention to its manifold utterances, as also to those of
his counterparts and of all the other characters involved.

(63)

To see what kinds of *Gestus* a play can embrace, let
us run through the opening scenes of a fairly modern
play, my own *Galileo*.[8] Since we wish at the same time to
find out what light the different utterances cast on one another we will assume that it is not our first introduction to
the play. It begins with the man of forty-six having his
morning wash, broken by occasional browsing in books and
by a lesson on the solar system for Andrea Sarti, a small
boy. In order to play this, surely you have got to know
that we shall be ending with the man of seventy-eight
having his supper, just after he has said good-by forever
to the same pupil. He is then more terribly altered than
this passage of time could possibly have brought about.
He wolfs his food with unrestrained greed, no other idea
in his head; he has rid himself of his educational mission
in shameful circumstances, as though it were a burden: he,
who once drank his morning milk without a care, greedy
to teach the boy. But does he really drink it without care?
Isn't the pleasure of drinking and washing all one with the
pleasure which he takes in the new ideas? Don't forget:
he thinks out of self-indulgence. . . . Is that good or bad?
I would advise you to represent it as good, since on this
point you will find nothing in the whole play to harm society, and more especially because you yourself are, I
hope, a gallant child of the scientific age. But take careful note: many horrible things will happen in this connection. The fact that the man who here acclaims the new

[8] Charles Laughton's English version is to be found in my
anthology, *From the Modern Repertoire*, Series Two, Denver,
1952 (and since 1953 distributed by the Indiana University
Press) (E. B.).

age will be forced at the end to beg this age to disown him
as contemptible, even to dispossess him—all this is one
relevant point. As for the lesson, you may like to decide
whether the man's heart is so full that his mouth is over-
flowing, so that he has to talk to anybody about it, even
a child, or whether the child must first draw the knowledge
out of him, by knowing him and showing interest. Again,
there may be two of them who cannot restrain themselves,
the one from asking, the other from giving the answer: a
bond of this sort would be interesting, for one day it is
going to be rudely snapped. Of course you will want the
demonstration of the earth's rotation round the sun to
be conducted quickly, since it is given for nothing, and
now the wealthy unknown pupil appears, lending the scholar's time a monetary value. He shows no interest, but he has
to be served; Galileo lacks resources, so he will stand between the wealthy pupil and the intelligent one, and sigh as
he makes his choice. There is little that he can teach
his new student, and so he learns from him instead; he
hears of the telescope which has been invented in Holland:
in his own way he gets something out of the disturbance
of his morning's work. The Rector of the university arrives.
Galileo's application for an increase in salary has been
turned down; the university is reluctant to pay as much
for the theories of physics as for those of theology; it
wishes him, who after all is operating on a generally accepted low level of scholarship, to produce something useful here and now. You will see from the way in which he
offers his treatise that he is used to being refused and
corrected. The Rector reminds him that the Republic
guarantees freedom of research even if she doesn't pay;
he replies that he cannot make much of this freedom if
he lacks the leisure which good payment permits. Here
you should not find his impatience too peremptory, or
his poverty will not be given due weight. For shortly after
that you find him having ideas which need some explanation; the prophet of a new age of scientific truth considers
how he can trick the Republic by offering her the telescope
as his own invention. All he sees in the new invention, you
will be surprised to hear, is a few scudi, and he examines
it simply with a view to annexing it for himself. But if you
move on to the second scene, you will find that while he
is selling the invention to the Venetian *signoria* with a
speech that disgraces him by its falsehoods he has al-

ready almost forgotten the money, for he has realized
that the instrument has not only military but astronomical
significance. The article which he has been blackmailed
—let us call it that—into producing proves to have great
qualities for the very research which he had to break off
in order to produce it. If during the ceremony, as he com-
placently accepts the undeserved honors paid him, he
outlines to his learned friend the marvelous discoveries in
view—don't overlook the theatrical way in which he does
this—you will find in him a far more profound excitement
than the thought of monetary gain called forth. Seen in
this light, his charlatanry may not mean much, but it
still shows how determined the man is to take the easy
course, and to apply his reason in a base as well as a noble
way. A more significant test awaits him; and does not
every capitulation bring the next one closer?

(64)

Splitting such material into one *Gestus* after another,
the actor masters his character by first mastering the
story.[9] It is only after walking all around the entire episode
that he can, as it were by a single leap, seize and fix his
character, complete with all its individual features. Once
he has done his utmost to let himself be amazed by the inconsistencies in its various attitudes, knowing that he in
turn will have to make them amaze the audience, then the
story considered as a whole may allow him to pull the inconsistencies together; for the story, being a clearly defined episode, has a specific sense, i.e., only gratifies
a specific fraction of all the interests that might arise.

(65)

Everything hangs on the story; it is the heart of the
theatrical performance. For it is what happens *between*
people that provides them with the material to discuss,
criticize, alter. Even if the particular person represented by the actor has ultimately to fit into more than
just the one episode, it is mainly because the episode
will be all the more striking if it reaches fulfillment in a
particular person. The story is the theatre's great opera-

---

[9] Brecht's word is "Fabel"—the Latin *Fabula* (E. B.).

tion: the whole complex of incidents with each different *Gestus*, embracing the communications and impulses that must now go to make up the audience's entertainment.

(66)

Each single incident has its basic *Gestus: Richard Gloster courts his victim's widow. The child's true mother is found by means of a chalk circle. God has a bet with the Devil for Dr. Faustus' soul. Woyzeck buys a cheap knife in order to do in his wife,* etc. The grouping of the characters on the stage and the movements of the groups must be such that the necessary beauty is attained above all by the elegance with which the material conveying that *Gestus* is set out and laid bare to the understanding of the audience.

(67)

As we cannot invite the audience to fling itself into the story as if it were a river and let itself be carried vaguely hither and thither, the individual episodes have to be knotted together in such a way that the knots are easily noticed. The episodes must not succeed one another in-distinguishably but must give us a chance to interpose our judgment. (If it were above all the obscurity of the original interrelations that interested us, then this circum-stance would have to be made sufficiently strange.) The parts of the story have to be carefully set off one against another by giving each its own structure as a play within the play. To this end it is best to agree to use titles like those in the preceding paragraph. The titles must include the social point, saying at the same time something about the kind of portrayal wanted, i.e., should copy the tone of a chronicle or a ballad or a newspaper or a morality. For instance, a simple way of making something seem un-familiar is that which is normally applied to customs and moral principles. A visit, the treatment of an enemy, a lovers' meeting, agreements about politics or business, can be portrayed as though they were simply illustrations of general principles valid for the place in question. Shown thus, the particular and unrepeatable incident acquires a disconcerting look, because it appears as something general, something that has become a principle. As soon as we ask whether in fact it should have become such, or what about it should have done so, we are treating the incident as unfamiliar. The poetic approach to history can be studied in the so-called panoramas at sideshows in fairs. Since this detached treatment means lending historical perspective, certain incidents can just be represented as historic, as though they had for a long while been common knowledge and care must be taken not to offer the least obstacle to their further transmission. In short, there are many conceivable ways of telling a story, some of them known and some still waiting to be discovered.

(68)

What needs to be treated as unfamiliar, and how this is to be done, depends on the exposition demanded by the entire episode; and this is where the theatre has to speak up decisively for the interests of its own time. Let us take as an example of such exposition the old play *Hamlet*. Given the dark and bloody period in which I am writing—the criminal ruling classes, the widespread doubt in the power of reason, continually being misused— I think that I can read the story thus: It is an age of warriors. Hamlet's father, King of Denmark, slew the King of Norway in a successful war of spoliation. While the latter's son Fortinbras is arming for a fresh war, the Danish king is likewise slain—by his own brother. The slain kings' brothers, now themselves kings, avert war by arranging that the Norwegian troops should cross Danish soil to launch a predatory war against Poland. But at this point the young Hamlet is summoned by his warrior father's ghost to avenge the crime committed against him. After at first being reluctant to answer one bloody deed by another, and even preparing to go into exile, he meets young Fortinbras at the coast as he is marching with his troops to Poland. Overcome by this warrior-like example, he turns back[10] and in a piece of barbaric butchery slaughters his uncle, his mother, and himself, leaving Denmark to the

---

[10] But Hamlet in fact does not turn back at that point, nor is it accurate to say that he slaughters his mother and himself. When I made some such comments to Brecht, he replied with the following letter, only part of which has previously been published (in Beatrice Gottlieb's translation of the *Organum*, *Accent*, Urbana, 1951):

Norwegian. These events show the young man, already somewhat stout, making the most ineffective use of the new approach to Reason which he has picked up at the University of Wittenberg. In the feudal business to which he returns it simply hampers him. Faced with irrational practices, his reason is utterly unpractical. He falls a tragic victim to the discrepancy between such reasoning and such action. This way of reading the play, which can be read in more than one way, might in my view interest our audience.

(69)

Whether or no literature presents them as successes, each step forward, every emancipation from nature that is scored in the field of production so as to lead to a

---

Berliner Ensemble
Berlin N.W. 7
31 October, 1949

Dear Bentley,

You are right. Section 68 of the *Short Organum* needs a footnote and a correction.

Correction: Instead of "and in a piece of barbaric butchery slaughters his uncle, his mother, and himself," it must read: "and in a piece of barbaric butchery brings about the death of his uncle, his mother, and himself."

Footnote: The fourth scene of the Fourth Act (A plain in Denmark), in which we see Hamlet for the last time before his return in the flesh, we take to be the turning point. Here he has the great monologue in which he succumbs to Fortinbras' drums of war: "Oh, from this time forth/ My thoughts be bloody or be nothing worth!" True, the letter to Horatio in the scene after next announces that Hamlet has nonetheless taken ship for England. But none of this is acted out, and his report to Horatio on the king's plot against him (II, 2) [*sic.* But V, 2 must be meant.—E. B.] does not give the performer the chance to enact his decision (to go to England).

The Hamlet interpretation is just an example of an *interpretation*—that is, certain emphases and displacements, possibly cuts, and even occasionally (not in this case) interpolations are needed.

Anyhow the *Short Organum* will be read here for the moment chiefly by students. To be sure, more discussion is under way about my demand that the theatres should use our Model Books. You know, of course, the *Antigone* Model, and now Suhrkamp is bringing out the *Courage* Model. And I have also prepared an example of a text on The Building of a Role—Laughton's *Galilei*.

I'd be very glad if you could come over to this side again this winter. Unhappily we cannot do anything for you in the Golden West. Warmly, Your Brecht. (E. B.).

transformation of society, all those explorations in some
new direction which mankind has embarked on in order to
improve its lot, give us a sense of confidence and triumph
and lead us to take pleasure in the possibilities of change
in all things. Galileo expresses this when he says: "It is
my view that the earth is most noble and wonderful, seeing the great number and variety of changes and generations which incessantly take place on it."

(70)

The exposition of the story and its communication by
suitable means of estrangement constitute the main business of the theatre. Not everything depends on the actor,
even though nothing may be done without taking him into
account. The story is set out, brought forward, and
shown by the theatre as a whole, by actors, stage designers,
mask-makers, costumers, composers, and choreographers.
They unite their various arts for the joint operation, without of course sacrificing their independence in the process.

(71)

It emphasizes the general *Gestus* of showing, which
always underlies that which is being shown, when the audience is musically addressed by means of songs. Because
of this the actors ought not to "drop into" song, but
should clearly mark it off from the rest of the text; and
this is best reinforced by a few theatrical methods such
as changing the lighting or inserting a title. For its part,
the music must strongly resist the smooth incorporation
which is generally expected of it and turns it into an un-
thinking slavey. Music does not "accompany" except in the
form of comment. It cannot simply "express itself" by
discharging the emotions with which the incidents of the
play have filled it. Thus Eisler, e.g., helped admirably in
the knotting of the incidents when in the carnival scene
of *Galileo* he set the masked procession of the guilds to
a triumphant and threatening music which showed what
a revolutionary twist the lower orders had given to the
scholar's astronomical theories. Similarly in *The Caucasian
Chalk Circle*[11] the singer, by using a chilly and unemo-

[11] *The Caucasian Chalk Circle* is to be found in the volume
Parables for the Theatre, University of Minnesota Press, 1948
(and since 1957 an Evergreen Paperback) (E. B.).

tional way of singing to describe the servant girl's rescue of the child as it is being mimed on the stage, makes plain the terror of a period in which motherly instincts can become a suicidal weakness. Thus music can make its point in a number of ways and with full independence, and can give its own reaction to the subjects dealt with; at the same time it can also quite simply help to lend variety to the entertainment.

(72)

Just as the composer wins back his freedom by no longer having to create an atmosphere which allows the audience to lose itself unreservedly in the events on the stage, so also the stage designer gets considerable freedom as soon as he no longer needs to give the illusion of a room or a locality when he is building his sets. It is enough for him to give hints, though these must make statements of greater historical or social interest than does the real setting. At the Jewish Theatre in Moscow *King Lear* was rendered unfamiliar by a structure that recalled a medieval tabernacle; Neher set *Galileo* in front of projections of maps, documents, and Renaissance works of art; for *Haitang Erwacht* at the Piscator-Theater in Berlin Heartfield used a background of reversible flags bearing inscriptions, to mark changes in the political situation of which the persons on the stage were sometimes unaware.

(73)

For choreography, too, there are once again tasks of a realistic kind. It is a relatively recent error to suppose that it has nothing to do with the representation of "people as they really are." If art reflects life it does so with special mirrors. Art does not become unrealistic by changing the proportions but by changing them in such a way that if the audience took its representations as a practical guide to insights and impulses it would go astray in real life. It is of course essential that stylization should not remove the natural element but should heighten it. Anyhow, a theatre where everything depends on the *Gestus* cannot do without choreography. Elegant movement and graceful grouping, for a start, promote detachment, and inventive miming greatly helps the story.

(74)

So let us invite all the sister arts of the drama, not in order to create an "integrated work of art" (*Gesamtkunstwerk*) in which they all offer themselves up and are lost, but so that together with the drama they may further the common task in their different ways; and their relations with one another consist in this: that they lead to mutual detachment.

(75)

And here once again let us recall that their task is to entertain the children of the scientific age, and to do so with sensuousness and humor. This is something that we Germans cannot tell ourselves too often, for with us everything easily slips into the insubstantial and unapproachable, and we begin to talk of a World View (*Weltanschauung*) when the world in question has already dissolved. Even materialism is little more than an idea with us. Sexual pleasure with us turns into marital obligations, the pleasures of art subserve culture, and by learning we mean not an enjoyable process of finding out, but the forcible shoving of our nose into something. Our activity has none of the pleasure of exploration, and if we want to make our mark we do not say how much fun we have got out of something but how much effort it has cost us.

(76)

One more thing: the delivery to the audience of what has been built up in the rehearsals. Here it is essential that the actual playing should be infused with the *Gestus* of handing over a finished article. What now comes before the spectator is the most frequently repeated of what has not been rejected, and so the finished representations have to be delivered with the eyes fully open, so that they may be received with the eyes open too.

(77)

That is to say, our representations must take second place to what is represented—people's life together in society—and the pleasure felt in their perfection must be converted into the higher pleasure felt when the rules emerging from this life in society are treated as imperfect and provisional. In this way the theatre leaves its spectators productively disposed even after the spectacle is over. Let us hope that their theatre may allow them to enjoy as entertainment that terrible and never-ending labor which should insure their maintenance, together with the terror of their unceasing transformation. Let them here produce their own lives in the simplest way; for the simplest way of living is in art.

THORNTON WILDER
(b. 1897)

Some Thoughts on Playwriting[1] (1941)

FOUR FUNDAMENTAL conditions of the drama separate it from the other arts. Each of these conditions has its advantages and disadvantages, each requires a particular aptitude from the dramatist, and from each there are a number of instructive consequences to be derived. These conditions are:

1. The theatre is an art which reposes upon the work of many collaborators;

2. It is addressed to the group-mind;

3. It is based upon a pretense and its very nature calls out a multiplication of pretenses;

4. Its action takes place in a perpetual present time.

I. THE THEATRE IS AN ART WHICH REPOSES UPON THE WORK OF MANY COLLABORATORS

We have been accustomed to think that a work of art is by definition the product of one governing selecting will.

A landscape by Cézanne consists of thousands of brushstrokes each commanded by one mind. *Paradise Lost* and *Pride and Prejudice*, even in cheap frayed copies, bear the immediate and exclusive message of one intelligence.

It is true that in musical performance we meet with intervening executants, but the element of intervention is slight compared to that which takes place in drama. Illustrations:

1. One of the finest productions of *The Merchant of Venice* in our time showed Sir Henry Irving as Shylock, a noble, wronged, and indignant being, of such stature

[1] Thornton Wilder, "Some Thoughts on Playwriting," in *The Intent of the Artist*, edited by Augusto Centeno. Copyright Princeton University Press, 1941, pp. 83–98.

that the Merchants of Venice dwindled before him into irresponsible schoolboys. He was confronted in court by a gracious, even queenly, Portia, Miss Ellen Terry. At the Odéon in Paris, however, Gémier played Shylock as a vengeful and hysterical buffoon, confronted in court by a Portia who was a *gamine* from the Paris streets with a lawyer's quill three feet long over her ear; at the close of the trial scene Shylock was driven screaming about the auditorium, behind the spectators' back and onto the stage again, in a wild Elizabethan revel. Yet for all their divergences both were admirable productions of the play.

2. If there were ever a play in which fidelity to the author's requirements were essential in the representation of the principal role, it would seem to be Ibsen's *Hedda Gabler,* for the play is primarily an exposition of her character. Ibsen's directions read: "Enter from the left Hedda Gabler. She is a woman of twenty-nine. Her face and figure show great refinement and distinction. Her complexion is pale and opaque. Her steel-gray eyes express an unruffled calm. Her hair is of an attractive medium brown, but is not particularly abundant; and she is dressed in a flowing loose-fitting morning gown." I once saw Eleonora Duse in this role. She was a woman of sixty and made no effort to conceal it. Her complexion was pale and transparent. Her hair was white, and she was dressed in a gown that suggested some medieval empress in mourning. And the performance was very fine.

One may well ask: why write for the theatre at all? Why not work in the novel where such deviations from one's intentions cannot take place?

There are two answers:

1. The theatre presents certain vitalities of its own so inviting and stimulating that the writer is willing to receive them in compensation for this inevitable variation from an exact image.

2. The dramatist through working in the theatre gradually learns not merely to take account of the presence of the collaborators, but to derive advantage from them; and he learns, above all, to organize the play in such a way that its strength lies not in appearances beyond his control, but in the succession of events and in the unfolding of an idea, in narration.

The gathered audience sits in a darkened room, one end of which is lighted. The nature of the transaction

at which it is gazing is a succession of events illustrating
a general idea — the stirring of the idea; the gradual
feeding out of information; the shock and countershock
of circumstances; the flow of action; the interruption of
action; the moments of allusion to earlier events; the
preparation of surprise, dread, or delight — all that is
the author's and his alone.

For reasons to be discussed later — the expectancy
of the group-mind, the problem of time on the stage, the
absence of the narrator, the element of pretense — the
theatre carries the art of narration to a higher power
than the novel or the epic poem. The theatre is unfolding action and in the disposition of events the authors
may exercise a governance so complete that the distor-
tions effected by the physical appearance of actors, by
the fancies of scene painters and the misunderstandings
of directors, fall into relative insignificance. It is just
because the theatre is an art of many collaborators, with
the constant danger of grave misinterpretation, that the
dramatist learns to turn his attention to the laws of narration, its logic and its deep necessity of presenting a
unifying idea stronger than its mere collection of happenings. The dramatist must be by instinct a storyteller.

There is something mysterious about the endowment of
the storyteller. Some very great writers possessed very
little of it, and some others, lightly esteemed, possessed
it in so large a measure that their books survive down the
ages, to the confusion of severer critics. Alexandre Dumas
had it to an extraordinary degree; while Melville, for all
his splendid quality, had it barely sufficiently to raise his
work from the realm of non-fiction. It springs, not, as some
have said, from an aversion to general ideas, but from an
instinctive coupling of idea and illustration; the idea, for
a born storyteller, can only be expressed imbedded in
its circumstantial illustration. The myth, the parable,
the fable are the fountainhead of all fiction and in them
is seen most clearly the didactic, moralizing employment
of a story. Modern taste shrinks from emphasizing the central idea that hides behind the fiction, but it exists there
nevertheless, supplying the unity to fantasizing, and
offering a justification to what otherwise we would repudi-
ate as mere arbitrary contrivance, pretentious lying, or in-
dividualistic emotional association spinning. For all their
magnificent intellectual endowment, George Meredith

and George Eliot were not born storytellers; they chose
fiction as the vehicle for their reflections, and the passing
of time is revealing their error in that choice. Jane Austen
was pure storyteller and her works are outlasting those
of apparently more formidable rivals. The theatre is
more exacting than the novel in regard to this faculty,
and its presence constitutes a force which compensates
the dramatist for the deviations which are introduced into
his work by the presence of his collaborators.

The chief of these collaborators are the actors.

The actor's gift is a combination of three separate
faculties or endowments. Their presence to a high degree in any one person is extremely rare, although the
ambition to possess them is common. Those who rise
to the height of the profession represent a selection and
a struggle for survival in one of the most difficult and
cruel of the artistic activities. The three endowments
that compose the gift are observation, imagination, and
physical co-ordination.

1. An observant and analyzing eye for all modes of
behavior about us, for dress and manner, and for the
signs of thought and emotion in one's self and in others.

2. The strength of imagination and memory whereby
the actor may, at the indication in the author's text,
explore his store of observations and represent the details of appearance and the intensity of the emotions —
joy, fear, surprise, grief, love, and hatred, and through
imagination extend them to intenser degrees and to
differing characterizations.

3. A physical co-ordination whereby the force of
these inner realizations may be communicated to voice,
face, and body.

An actor must *know* the appearances and the mental
states; he must *apply* his knowledge to the role; and he
must physically *express* his knowledge. Moreover, his
concentration must be so great that he can effect this
representation under conditions of peculiar difficulty —
in abrupt transition from the non-imaginative conditions behind the stage; and in the presence of fellow-
actors who may be momentarily destroying the reality
of the action.

A dramatist prepares the characterization of his personages in such a way that it will take advantage of the
actor's gift.

Characterization in a novel is presented by the author's dogmatic assertion that the personage was such, and by an analysis of the personage with generally an account of his or her past. Since, in the drama, this is replaced by the actual presence of the personage before us and since there is no occasion for the intervening all-knowing author to instruct us as to his or her inner nature, a far greater share is given in a play to (1) highly characteristic utterances and (2) concrete occasions in which the character defines itself under action and (3) a conscious preparation of the text whereby the actor may build upon the suggestions in the role according to his own abilities.

Characterization in a play is like a blank check which the dramatist accords to the actor for him to fill in — not entirely blank, for a number of indications of individuality are already there, but to a far less definite and absolute degree than in the novel.

The dramatist's principal interest being the movement of the story, he is willing to resign the more detailed aspects of characterization to the actor and is often rewarded beyond his expectation.

The sleepwalking scene from *Macbeth* is a highly compressed selection of words whereby despair and remorse rise to the surface of indirect confession. It is to be assumed that had Shakespeare lived to see what the genius of Sarah Siddons could pour into the scene from that combination of observation, self-knowledge, imagination, and representational skill, even he might have exclaimed, "I never knew I wrote so well!"

II. THE THEATRE IS AN ART ADDRESSED TO A GROUP-MIND

Painting, sculpture, and the literature of the book are certainly solitary experiences; and it is likely that most people would agree that the audience seated shoulder to shoulder in a concert hall is not an essential element in musical enjoyment.

But a play presupposes a crowd. The reasons for this go deeper than (1) the economic necessity for the support of the play and (2) the fact that the temperament of actors is proverbially dependent on group attention.

It rests on the fact that (1) the pretense, the fiction, on the stage would fall to pieces and absurdity without the support accorded to it by a crowd, and (2) the excitement induced by pretending a fragment of life is such that it partakes of ritual and festival, and requires a throng.

Similarly the fiction that royal personages are of a mysteriously different nature from other people requires audiences, levees, and processions for its maintenance. Since the beginnings of society, satirists have occupied themselves with the descriptions of kings and queens in their intimacy and delighted in showing how the prerogatives of royalty become absurd when the crowd is not present to extend to them the enhancement of an imaginative awe.

The theatre partakes of the nature of festival. Life imitated is life raised to a higher power. In the case of comedy, the vitality of these pretended surprises, deceptions, and *contretemps* becomes so lively that before a spectator, solitary or regarding himself as solitary, the structure of so much event would inevitably expose the artificiality of the attempt and ring hollow and unjustified; and in the case of tragedy, the accumulation of woe and apprehension would soon fall short of conviction. All actors know the disturbing sensation of playing before a handful of spectators at a dress rehearsal or performance where only their interest in pure craftsmanship can barely sustain them. During the last rehearsals the phrase is often heard: "This play is hungry for an audience."

Since the theatre is directed to a group-mind, a number of consequences follow:

1. A group-mind presupposes, if not a lowering of standards, a broadening of the fields of interest. The other arts may presuppose an audience of connoisseurs trained in leisure and capable of being interested in certain rarefied aspects of life. The dramatist may be prevented from exhibiting, for example, detailed representations of certain moments in history that require specialized knowledge in the audience, or psychological states in the personages which are of insufficient general interest to evoke self-identification in the majority. In the Second Part of Goethe's *Faust* there are long passages dealing with the theory of paper money. The exposition of the nature of misanthropy (so much more drastic than Molière's) in Shakespeare's *Timon of Athens* has never been a suc-

cess. The dramatist accepts this limitation in subject matter and realizes that the group-mind imposes upon him the necessity of treating material understandable by the larger number.

2. It is the presence of the group-mind that brings another requirement to the theatre—forward movement.

Maeterlinck said that there was more drama in the spectacle of an old man seated by a table than in the majority of plays offered to the public. He was juggling with the various meanings in the word "drama." In the sense whereby drama means the intensified concentration of life's diversity and significance he may well have been right; if he meant drama as a theatrical representation before an audience he was wrong. Drama on the stage is inseparable from forward movement, from action.

Many attempts have been made to present Plato's dialogues, Gobineau's fine series of dialogues, *La Renaissance,* and the *Imaginary Conversations* of Landor; but without success. Through some ingredient in the group-mind, and through the sheer weight of anticipation involved in the dressing up and the assumption of fictional roles, an action is required, and an action that is more than a mere progress in argumentation and debate.

III. THE THEATRE IS A WORLD OF PRETENSE

It lives by conventions: a convention is an agreed-upon falsehood, a permitted lie.

Illustrations: Consider at the first performance of the *Medea,* the passage where Medea meditates the murder of her children. An anecdote from antiquity tells us that the audience was so moved by this passage that considerable disturbance took place.

The following conventions were involved:

1. Medea was played by a man.

2. He wore a large mask on his face. In the lip of the mask was an acoustical device for projecting the voice. On his feet he wore shoes with soles and heels half a foot high.

3. His costume was so designed that it conveyed

to the audience, by convention: woman of royal birth and Oriental origin.

4. The passage was in metric speech. All poetry is an "agreed-upon falsehood" in regard to speech.

5. The lines were sung in a kind of recitative. All opera involves this "permitted lie" in regard to speech.

Modern taste would say that the passage would convey much greater pathos if a woman "like Medea" had delivered it — with an uncovered face that exhibited all the emotions she was undergoing. For the Greeks, however, there was no pretense that Medea was on the stage. The mask, the costume, the mode of declamation, were a series of signs which the spectator interpreted and reassembled in his own mind. Medea was being re-created within the imagination of each of the spectators.

The history of the theatre shows us that in its greatest ages the stage employed the greatest number of conventions. The stage is fundamental pretense and it thrives on the acceptance of that fact and in the multiplication of additional pretenses. When it tries to assert that the personages in the action "really are," really inhabit such and such rooms, really suffer such and such emotions, it loses rather than gains credibility. The modern world is inclined to laugh condescendingly at the fact that in the plays of Racine and Corneille the gods and heroes of antiquity were dressed like the courtiers under Louis XIV; that in the Elizabethan age scenery was replaced by placards notifying the audience of the location; and that a whip in the hand and a jogging motion of the body indicated that a man was on horseback in the Chinese theatre; these devices did not spring from naïveté, however, but from the vitality of the public imagination in those days and from an instinctive feeling as to where the essential and where the inessential lay in drama.

The convention has two functions:

1. It provokes the collaborative activity of the spectator's imagination; and

2. It raises the action from the specific to the general.

This second aspect is of even greater importance than the first.

If Juliet is represented as a girl "very like Juliet" — it was not merely a deference to contemporary prejudices that assigned this role to a boy in the Elizabethan age — moving about in a "real" house with marble staircases, rugs, lamps, and furniture, the impression is irresistibly conveyed that these events happened to this one girl, in one place, at one moment in time. When the play is staged as Shakespeare intended it, the bareness of the stage releases the events from the particular and the experience of Juliet partakes of that of all girls in love, in every time, place and language.

The stage continually strains to tell this generalized truth and it is the element of pretense that reinforces it. Out of the lie, the pretense, of the theatre proceeds a truth more compelling than the novel can attain, for the novel by its own laws is constrained to tell of an action that "once happened" — "once upon a time."

IV. THE ACTION ON THE STAGE TAKES PLACE IN A PERPETUAL PRESENT TIME

Novels are written in the past tense. The characters in them, it is true, are represented as living moment by moment their present time, but the constant running commentary of the novelist ("Tess slowly descended into the valley"; "Anna Karenina laughed") inevitably conveys to the reader the fact that these events are long since past and over.

The novel is a past reported in the present. On the stage it is always now. This confers upon the action an increased vitality which the novelist longs in vain to incorporate into his work.

This condition in the theatre brings with it another important element:

In the theatre we are not aware of the intervening storyteller. The speeches arise from the characters in an apparently pure spontaneity.

A play is what takes place.

A novel is what one person tells us took place.

A play visibly represents pure existing. A novel is what one mind, claiming to omniscience, asserts to have existed.

Many dramatists have regretted this absence of the narrator from the stage, with his point of view, his powers of analyzing the behavior of the characters, his ability to interfere and supply further facts about the past, about simultaneous actions not visible on the stage, and above *all* his function of pointing the moral and emphasizing the significance of the action. In some periods of the theatre he has been present as chorus, or prologue and epilogue or as *raisonneur*. But surely this absence constitutes an additional force to the form, as well as an additional tax upon the writer's skill. It is the task of the dramatist so to co-ordinate his play, through the selection of episodes and speeches, that, though he is himself not visible, his point of view and his governing intention will impose themselves on the spectator's attention, not as dogmatic assertion or motto, but as self-evident truth and inevitable deduction.

Imaginative narration — the invention of souls and destinies — is to a philosopher an all but indefensible activity.

Its justification lies in the fact that the communication of ideas from one mind to another inevitably reaches the point where exposition passes into illustration, into parable, metaphor, allegory, and myth.

It is no accident that when Plato arrived at the height of his argument and attempted to convey a theory of knowledge and a theory of the structure of man's nature he passed over into story telling, into the myths of the Cave and the Charioteer; and that the great religious teachers have constantly had recourse to the parable as a means of imparting their deepest intuitions.

The theatre offers to imaginative narration its highest possibilities. It has many pitfalls and its very vitality betrays it into service as mere diversion and the enhancement of insignificant matter; but it is well to remember that it was the theatre that rose to the highest place during those epochs that aftertime has chosen to call "great ages" and that the Athens of Pericles and the reigns of Elizabeth, Philip II, and Louis XIV were also the ages that gave to the world the greatest dramas it has known.

Forgers of Myths[1] (1946)

IN READING the newspaper reviews of Katharine Cornell's
production of Jean Anouilh's *Antigone,* I had the impression that the play had created a certain amount of
discomfort in the minds of the New York drama critics.
Many expressed surprise that such an ancient myth should
be staged at all. Others reproached Antigone with being
neither alive nor credible, with not having what, in theatre
jargon, is called "character." The misunderstanding, I
believe, was due to the fact that the critics were not
informed of what many young authors in France—each
along differing lines and without concerted aim—are at-
tempting to do.

There has been a great deal of discussion in France
about "a return to tragedy," about the "rebirth of the
philosophic play." The two labels are confusing and they
should both be rejected. Tragedy is, for us, an historic
phenomenon which flourished between the sixteenth and
eighteenth centuries; we have no desire to begin that over
again. Nor are we anxious to produce philosophic plays,
if by that is meant works deliberately intended to set
forth on the stage the philosophy of Marx, St. Thomas,
or existentialism. Nevertheless there is some truth at-
tached to these two labels: in the first place, it is a fact
that we are less concerned with making innovations than
with returning to a tradition; it is likewise true that the
problems we wish to deal with in the theatre are very
different from those we habitually dealt with before 1940.

The theatre, as conceived of in the period between the

[1] Jean-Paul Sartre, "Forgers of Myths," translated by Rosa-
mond Gilder, *Theatre Arts Anthology,* edited by Rosamond
Gilder, Hermine Rich Isaacs and others (New York: Theatre
Arts Books, 1951), pp. 135–42. Copyright 1946 by Theatre
Arts, Inc., 1950 by Theatre Arts Books.

two world wars, and as it is perhaps still thought of in the United States today, is a theatre of characters. The analysis of characters and their confrontation was the theatre's chief concern. The so-called "situations" existed only for the purpose of throwing the characters into clearer relief. The best plays in this period were psychological studies of a coward, a liar, an ambitious man or a frustrated one. Occasionally a playwright made an effort to outline the workings of a passion—usually love—or to analyze an inferiority complex.

Judged by such principles Anouilh's Antigone is not a character at all. Nor is she simply a peg on which to hang a passion calculated to develop along the approved lines of whatever psychology might be in style. She represents a naked will, a pure, free choice; in her there is no distinguishing between passion and action. The young playwrights of France do not believe that men share a ready-made "human nature" which may alter under the impact of a given situation. They do not think that individuals can be seized with a passion or a mania which can be explained purely on the grounds of heredity, environment, and situations. What is universal, to their way of thinking, is not nature but the situations in which man finds himself; that is, not the sum total of his psychological traits but the limits which enclose him on all sides.

For them man is not to be defined as a "reasoning animal," or a "social" one, but as a free being, entirely indeterminate, who must choose his own being when confronted with certain necessities, such as being already committed in a world full of both threatening and favorable factors among other men who have made their choices before him, who have decided in advance the meaning of those factors. He is faced with the necessity of having to work and die, of being hurled into a life already complete which yet is his own enterprise and in which he can never have a second chance; where he must play his cards and take risks no matter what the cost. That is why we feel the urge to put on the stage certain situations which throw light on the main aspects of the condition of man and to have the spectator participate in the free choice which man makes in these situations.

Thus, Anouilh's Antigone may have seemed abstract because she was not portrayed as a young Greek princess, formed by certain influences and some ghastly memories,

but rather as a free woman without any features at
all until she chooses them for herself in the moment
when she asserts her freedom to die despite the triumphant tyrant. Similarly, when the burgomaster of Vauxelles
in Simone de Beauvoir's *Les Bouches Inutiles* has to decide whether to save his beleaguered town by cutting off
half its citizens (women, children, and old men) or to
risk making them all perish in an effort to save them
all, we do not care whether he is sensual or cold,
whether he has an Oedipus complex, or whether he is
of an irritable or jolly disposition. No doubt if he is rash
or incautious, vain or pusillanimous, he will make the
wrong decision. But we are not interested in arranging
in advance the motivations or reasons which will inevitably force his choice. Rather, we are concerned in
presenting the anguish of a man who is both free and full
of good will, who in all sincerity is trying to find out
the side he must take, and who knows that when he
chooses the lot of others he is at the same time choosing
his own pattern of behavior and is deciding once and for
all whether he is to be a tyrant or a democrat.

If one of us happens to present character on the
boards, it is only for the purpose of getting rid of it at
once. For instance, Caligula, at the outset of Albert
Camus' play of that name, has a character. One is led
to believe he is gentle and well behaved, and no doubt
he actually is both. But that gentleness and that modesty
suddenly melt away in the face of the prince's horrifying
discovery of the world's absurdity. From then on he will
choose to be the man to persuade other men of that
absurdity, and the play becomes only the story of how
he carries out his purpose.

A man who is free within the circle of his own situations, who chooses, whether he wishes to or not, for
everyone else when he chooses for himself—that is
the subject matter of our plays. As a successor to the
theatre of characters we want to have a theatre of
situation; our aim is to explore all the situations that are
most common to human experience, those which occur
at least once in the majority of lives. The people in our
plays will be distinct from one another—not as a coward
is from a miser or a miser from a brave man, but rather
as actions are divergent or clashing, as right may con-

flict with right. In this it may well be said that we derive from the Corneillean tradition.

It is easy to understand, therefore, why we are not greatly concerned with psychology. We are not searching for the right "word" which will suddenly reveal the whole unfolding of a passion, nor yet the "act" which will seem most lifelike and inevitable to the audience. For us psychology is the most abstract of the sciences because it studies the workings of our passions without plunging them back into their true human surroundings, without their background of religious and moral values, the taboos and commandments of society, the conflicts of nations and classes, of rights, of wills, of actions. For us a man is a whole enterprise in himself. And passion is a part of that enterprise.

In this we return to the concept of tragedy as the Greeks saw it. For them, as Hegel has shown, passion was never a simple storm of sentiment but fundamentally always the assertion of a right. The fascism of Creon, the stubbornness of Antigone for Sophocles and Anouilh, the madness of Caligula for Camus, are *at one and the same time* transports of feeling which have their origin deep within us and expressions of impregnable will which are affirmations of systems of values and rights such as the rights of citizenship, the rights of the family, individual ethics, collective ethics, the right to kill, the right to reveal to human beings their pitiable condition, and so forth. We do not reject psychology, that would be absurd; we integrate life.

For fifty years one of the most celebrated subjects for dissertation in France has been formulated as follows: "Comment on La Bruyère's saying: Racine draws man as he is; Corneille, as he should be." We believe the statement should be reversed. Racine paints psychologic man, he studies the mechanics of love, of jealousy in an abstract, pure way; that is, without ever allowing moral considerations or human will to deflect the inevitability of their evolution. His dramatis personae are only creatures of his mind, the end results of an intellectual analysis. Corneille, on the other hand, showing will at the very core of passion, gives us back man in all his complexity, in his complete reality.

The young authors I am discussing take their stand on

Corneille's side. For them the theatre will be able to present man in his entirety only in proportion to the theatre's willingness to be *moral*. By that we do not mean that it should put forward examples illustrating the rules of deportment or the practical ethics taught to children, but rather that the study of the conflict of characters should be replaced by the presentation of the conflict of rights. It was not a question of the opposition of *character* between a Stalinist and a Trotskyite; it was not in their characters that an anti-Nazi of 1933 clashed with an S.S. guard; the difficulties in international politics do not derive from the characters of the men leading us; the strikes in the United States do not reveal conflicts of character between industrialists and workers. In each case it is, in the final analysis and in spite of divergent interests, the system of values, of ethics and of concepts of man which are lined up against each other.

Therefore, our new theatre definitely has drawn away from the so-called "realistic theatre" because "realism" has always offered plays made up of stories of defeat, laissez-faire, and drifting; it has always preferred to show how external forces batter a man to pieces, destroy him bit by bit, and ultimately make of him a weathervane turning with every change of wind. But we claim for ourselves the *true* realism because we know it is impossible, in everyday life, to distinguish between fact and right, the real from the ideal, psychology from ethics.

This theatre does not give its support to any one "thesis" and is not inspired by any preconceived idea. All it seeks to do is to explore the state of man in its entirety and to present to the modern man a portrait of himself, his problems, his hopes, and his struggles. We believe our theatre would betray its mission if it portrayed individual personalities, even if they were as universal types as a miser, a misanthrope, a deceived husband, because, if it is to address the masses, the theatre must speak in terms of their most general preoccupations, dispelling their anxieties in the form of myths which anyone can understand and feel deeply.

My first experience in the theatre was especially fortunate. When I was a prisoner in Germany in 1940, I wrote, staged, and acted in a Christmas play which, while pulling wool over the eyes of the German censor by means of simple symbols, was addressed to my fellow-prisoners. This drama, biblical in appearance only, was written and put on by a prisoner, was acted by prisoners in scenery painted by prisoners; it was aimed exclusively at prisoners (so much so that I have never since then permitted it to be staged or even printed), and it addressed them on the subject of their concerns as prisoners. No doubt it was neither a good play nor well acted: the work of an amateur, the critics would say, a product of special circumstances. Nevertheless, on this occasion, as I addressed my comrades across the footlights, speaking to them of their state as prisoners, when I suddenly saw them so remarkably silent and attentive, I realized what theatre ought to be—a great collective, religious phenomenon.

To be sure, I was, in this case, favored by special circumstances; it does not happen every day that your public is drawn together by one great common interest, a great loss or a great hope. As a rule, an audience is made up of the most diverse elements; a big businessman sits beside a traveling salesman or a professor, a man next to a woman, and each is subject to his own particular preoccupations. Yet this situation is a challenge to the playwright: he must create his public, he must fuse all the disparate elements in the auditorium into a single unity by awakening in the recesses of their spirits the things which all men of a given epoch and community care about.

This does not mean that our authors intend to make use of symbols in the sense that symbols are the expression either indirect or poetic of a reality one either cannot or will not grasp directly. We would feel a profound distaste today for representing happiness as an elusive bluebird, as Maeterlinck did. Our times are too austere for child's play of that sort. Yet if we reject the theatre of symbols, we still want ours to be one of myths; we want to attempt to show the public the great myths of death, exile, love. The characters in Albert Camus' *Le Malentendu* are not symbols, they are flesh and blood: *a* mother and *a* daughter, *a* son who comes back from a long journey; their tragic experiences are complete in themselves. And yet they are mythical in the sense that the misunderstanding which separates them can serve as the embodiment of all misunderstandings which separate man from himself, from the world, from other men.

The French public makes no mistake about this, as has been proved by the discussions engendered by certain plays. With *Les Bouches Inutiles,* for instance, criticism was not confined to discussing the story of the play which was based on actual events that took place frequently in the Middle Ages: it recognized in the play a condemnation of fascist procedures. The Communists, on the other hand, saw in it a condemnation of their own procedures: "The conclusion," so they said in their newspapers, "is couched in terms of petty bourgeois idealism. All useless mouths should have been sacrificed to save the city." Anouilh also stirred up a storm of discussion with *Antigone,* being charged on the one hand with being a Nazi, on the other with being an anarchist. Such violent reactions prove that our plays are reaching the public just where it is important that it should be reached.

Yet these plays are austere. To begin with, since the situation is what we care about above all, our theatre shows it at the very point where it is about to reach its climax. We do not take time out for learned research, we feel no need of registering the imperceptible evolution of a character or a plot: one does not reach death by degrees, one is suddenly confronted with it—and if one approaches politics or love by slow degrees, then acute problems, arising suddenly, call for no progression. By taking our dramatis personae and precipitating them, in the very first scene, into the highest pitch of their conflicts we turn to the well-known pattern of classic tragedy, which always seizes upon the action at the very moment it is headed for catastrophe.

Our plays are violent and brief, centered around one single event; there are few players and the story is compressed within a short space of time, sometimes only a few hours. As a result they obey a kind of "rule of the three unities," which has been only a little rejuvenated and modified. A single set, a few entrances, a few exits, intense arguments among the characters who defend their individual rights with passion—this is what sets our plays at a great distance from the brilliant fantasies of Broadway. Yet some of them find that their austerity and intensity have not lacked appreciation in Paris. Whether New York will like them is a question.

Since it is their aim to forge myths, to project for the audience an enlarged and enhanced image of its own sufferings, our playwrights turn their backs on the constant preoccupation of the realists, which is to reduce as far as possible the distance which separates the spectator from the spectacle. In 1942, in Gaston Baty's production of *The Taming of the Shrew*, there were steps going from the stage to the auditorium so that certain characters could go down among the orchestra seats. We are very far away from such concepts and methods. To us a play should not seem too *familiar*. Its greatness derives from its social and, in a certain sense, religious functions: it must remain a rite; even as it speaks to the spectators of themselves it must do it in a tone and with a constant reserve of manner which, far from breeding familiarity, will increase the distance between play and audience.

That is why one of our problems has been to search out a style of dialogue which, while utterly simple and made up of words on everyone's lips, will still preserve something of the ancient dignity of our tongue. We have all barred from our plays the digressions, the set speeches, and what we in France like to call the *"poésie de réplique"*; all this chitchat debases a language. It seems to us that we shall recapture a little of the pomp of ancient tragedies if we practice the most rigorous economy of words. As for me, in *Morts Sans Sépulture,* my latest play, I did not deny myself the use of familiar turns of phrase, swearwords, even slang, whenever I felt that such speech was germane to the characters. But I did attempt to preserve, through the pace of the dialogue, an extreme conciseness of statement—ellipses, brusque interruptions, a sort of inner tension in the phrases which at once set them apart from the easygoing sound of everyday talk. Camus' style in *Caligula* is different in kind but it is magnificently sober and taut. Simone de Beauvoir's language in *Les Bouches Inutiles* is so stripped that it is sometimes accused of dryness.

Dramas which are short and violent, sometimes reduced to the dimensions of a single long act (*Antigone* lasts an hour and a half, my own play, *Huis-Clos,* an hour and twenty minutes without intermission), dramas entirely centered on one event—usually a conflict of rights, bearing on some very general situation—written in a sparse, extremely tense style, with a small cast not presented for their individual characters but thrust into a conjunction where they are forced to make a choice— in brief this is the theatre, austere, moral, mythic, and ceremonial in aspect, which has given birth to new plays in Paris during the occupation and especially since the end of the war. They correspond to the needs of a people exhausted but tense, for whom liberation has not meant a return to abundance and who can live only with the utmost economy.

The very severity of these plays is in keeping with the severity of French life; their moral and metaphysical topics reflect the preoccupation of a nation which must at one and the same time reconstruct and re-create and which is searching for new principles. Are they the product of local circumstances or can their very austerity of form enable them to reach a wider public in more fortunate countries? This is a question we must ask ourselves frankly before we try to transplant them.

CHRISTOPHER FRY
(b. 1908)

Why Verse?[1] (1955)

. . . THERE ARE many people to whom verse in the theatre is an irritating, or boring, or distracting, or pretentious flight of fashion; and in certain moods I can pish and tush with the best of them. This point is not held so strongly about literature in general. It isn't often said that there should be no such thing as poetry at all. When Wordsworth writes:

> Felt in the blood, and felt along the heart

we should think twice, perhaps, before we asked him why he didn't write the passage in prose. "Felt in the blood, and felt along the heart" is a good example, by the way, of the speed and economy with which poetry can express what would take prose far longer.

What reason is there for limiting the theatre to one form of communication? It is even believed that the prose play and the verse play are in opposition, or that the one precludes the other; there appears to be a kind of color bar in the matter. Such rivalry is nonsense. Indeed, prose and verse existing side by side counter each other's dangers. If they pass altogether out of each other's reach they cease to be themselves, becoming on the one hand journalese, official cant, or any other string of sentences; and on the other, a vagueness, an abstraction, a preciousness. This interplay of difference, one touching the hand of the other as it separates, like men and women dancing the Grand Chain, is what keeps each in its own state of grace.

One explanation of our impatience with a verse play is that the spring of theatre is action, and any insistence upon words is felt to hang like heavy clothes on the body of an

1 Christopher Fry, "Why Verse?", *Vogue*, March, 1955, pp. 136–37. Copyright 1955 by Christopher Fry. Reprinted by permission of the author.

athlete. When we go to the theatre we go to be interested by a story of lives living out their conflicts in a concentration of time. We do not go to hear them discuss the matter; we go to see and hear them live it.

But we know that words and actions are not unrelated. One illuminates the other; and the full significance of action can be explored only by words. If we compare the murder of Maria Marten in the Red Barn, with the murder of Duncan in Macbeth's castle, we see that in each the physical action is roughly the same, but the significance of the action is entirely different. The one is merely done, the other is experienced, and the experience is in the words. What is more, the experience is the true nature of the action. The experience ultimately is the action. The action is not the dagger in Duncan's breast, or the blood on Macbeth's hand, but rather the limitless experience of the words arising out of them: the experience of

> Macbeth does murder sleep!

of:

> . . . this my hand will rather
> The multitudinous seas incarnadine,
> Making the green one red.

The three words "this my hand," in the context, so deepen our thoughts about the human hand and what it performs, that the action is not only true of this one human, and this one deed; it becomes also an elemental action, done in the beginning of the fallen world. In sounds alone, "multitudinous," which heaves like a wilderness of molten lava, set against the three monosyllables "this my hand," gives us, or should give us, an experience of being. We begin to feel there is not one action, but two, not two, but twenty in the course of a speech.

You may be prepared to agree with me that words give us a larger, or deeper, experience of action, but still you may say, "Why verse? Why this formality of syllables? Why this unnatural division of sentences into lines?"

I suggest we forget the questions, and go on as though verse plays, like wasps, are apparently with us for some reason which they don't reveal. I only ask you to allow me to suppose an organic discipline, pattern, or proportion in the universe, evident in all that we see, which is a government uniting the greatest with the least, form with behavior, natural event with historic event, which stamps its mark through us and through our perceptions, as the name of Brighton is marked through a stick of rock candy. When Milton says: "Elephants endors'd with towers," or when Wordsworth says: "A noticeable man with large gray eyes," they are not being so true to that organic discipline as, for instance, Chaucer, when he says:

> Now with his love, now in the colde grave
> Allone, withouten any companye.

I ask you to allow me to suppose a shaping but undogmatical presence "felt in the blood, and felt along the heart," which is of a kind with the law of gravity, and the moral law, and the law which gives us two legs and not six.

From the way I am going on you would think I was talking about the Eleusinian mysteries, not about a theatre in which you propose to spend an entertaining evening. It is the fault of the question "Why Verse?" I should really write a play which would be so good that the question would never arise, a play which would please not some of the people some of the time, but all of the people all of the time, which would be both the immediate appearance of things and the eternal nature of things, combined with felicity.

I wish I could promise any such thing. Every few generations have to shape afresh the language which will express both these things together; and some of us find, like the donkey, that communication with our fellow being is something not easily achieved. We may think we have avoided all misconception, and then overhear a member of the audience making his comment, as after a performance of *The Dark Is Light Enough* (a play about the Austro-Hungarian war, taking place near Vienna) when a gentleman said, with charitable resignation, "I never can understand these Russian plays."

It is no good asking poetry to tell us what it says; it simply *is* what it says. In the theatre it must have a direct surface meaning, an immediate impact of sense, but half its work should be going on below that meaning, drawing the ear, consciously or unconsciously, into a certain experience of being.

This has been an age of signposts, of ideologies, of patent cures, of battle cries; we must take up our positions, draw clear lines between this or that, label, analyze, dissect; we must live the letter, for the letter is the law. But we have been looking at the possibility that poetry has another, deeper law. The truth of poetry deepens under your eye. It is never absolute. There is no moment when we can trumpet it abroad as finally understood.

In a play I wrote called *A Sleep Of Prisoners,* Cain and Abel throw dice together, and Abel prays as he shakes the dice:

> Deal me high, deal me low
> Make my deeds
> My nameless needs.
> I know I do not know.

In our anxiety to be in the know we defend our scraps of knowledge and decision so passionately that over the centuries we have burned, tortured, imprisoned, shot, and blown up those who contradicted or doubted us. But the spirit of our scrap of knowledge was in the contradiction and doubt, as much as in the belief. What we were torturing and blowing up was the spirit of truth.

Poetry in the theatre is the action of listening. It is an unrolling exploration, following your nose, or it would be better to say following your ear, for sound itself, pure sound, has logic, as we know in music, and what does that logic accord to if not the universal discipline felt along the heart? What part this logic plays in our life here on the earth is beyond calculation. If it wakens harmony, modulation, and the resolving of discord in us, we are nearer to our proper natures.

> The man that hath no music in himself,
> Nor is not moved with concord of sweet sounds,
> Is fit for treasons, stratagems and spoils;
> The motions of his spirit are dull as night,
> And his affections dark as Erebus:
> Let no such man be trusted.
> Mark the music.

Mark the music. Even in the broad give-and-take of the theatre our ears should be able to accept the interplay of the vowel sounds of a line of poetry, and know them as indications of the universal discipline, and consider the comma in the line with almost as much purpose as the comma on the underwing of the butterfly. But this precision has to exist within the broad and tough character of the theatre; it has to hold its own against distractions of many kinds: against coughs in the auditorium, failings in the author, even—on rare occasions—against irregularities of the actor's memory; just as in life our awareness of our larger natures has to hold its own against a host of distractions within and without.

> Such harmony is in immortal souls;
> But whilst this muddy vesture of decay
> Doth grossly close it in, we can not hear it.

So the general lines of the play, the shape of the story, the disposition of the characters, should point and implicate by their actions and their wider uses the texture of the poetry. The large pattern of the action should have a meaning in itself, above and beyond the story; the kind of meaning which gives everlasting truth to myths and legends, and makes the fairy story into a sober fact; a meaning not so conscious as a parable or so contrived as an allegory, but as it were tracing a figure which the poetry can naturally and inevitably fill.

This is all very well, you may now say, this fine theory; but we have to put up with verse plays as they are, not as ideally they should be; it seems to us that a good deal of these plays could be written at least as well, and more honestly, in prose. Why, for instance, should you present to us as verse a speech such as this:

> I sometimes think
> His critical judgment is so exquisite
> It leaves us nothing to admire except his opinion.
> He should take into account
> The creative value of the fault.

I have no answer to satisfy you if you believe that human nature, or human personality, is divided into two parts, of whatever proportion, the prosaic and the poetic. I think we live always with a foot in each camp, or rather, that there is no moment when we can safely say that we belong entirely to one or the other. There is no moment when we can certainly say that even our apparently most insignificant actions have not a significance greatly beyond ourselves.

It is this tension between two meanings which verse conveys, favoring sometimes one, sometimes the other. The prosaic or colloquial can be rhythmically just sufficiently charged to resolve into the implication of verse at

a moment's notice, even halfway through a sentence, and
back again, without disturbing the unity of the speech,
in the way that the spirit and the flesh work in ourselves
without noticeably sawing us in half. The writer's responsibility is to know when he can safely break free of this,
and relax for contrast into the rhythms of prose.

In *The Dark Is Light Enough* there comes a moment
when the situation reduces everyone to silence; when
there seems no way of the scene going on without bringing
the curtain down. And then the Countess begins to speak.
I will tell you what she says, not because the verse does
what I want it to do, but it says something to our
purpose.

> How shall we manage, with time at a standstill?
> We can't go back to where nothing has been said;
> And no heart is served, caught in a moment
> Which has frozen. Since no words will set us free—
> Not at least now, until we can persuade
> Our thoughts to move—
> Music would unground us best,
> As a tide in the dark comes to boats at anchor
> And they begin to dance. My father told me
> How he went late one night, a night
> Of some Hungarian anxiety,
> To the Golden Bull at Buda, and there he found
> The President of your House of Deputies
> Alone and dancing in his shirtsleeves
> To the music of the band, himself
> Put far away, bewitched completely
> By the dance's custom; and so it went on,
> While my father drank and talked with friends,
> Three or four hours without a pause:
> This weighty man of seventy, whose whole
> Recognition of the world about him
> During those hours, was when occasionally
> He turned his eyes to the gipsy leader
> And the music changed, out of a comprehension
> As wordless as the music.
> It was dancing that came up out of the earth
> To take the old man's part against anxiety.

A comprehension as wordless as the music. It is this
comprehension which poetry tries to speak, this revelation
of discipline that comes up out of the earth, or is felt
along the heart; it is this which verse has to offer.

FRIEDRICH DUERRENMATT
(b. 1921)

Problems of the Theatre[1] (1955)

BEHOLD THE DRIVE for purity in art as art is practiced
these days. Behold this writer striving for the purely poetic, another for the purely lyrical, the purely epic, the
purely dramatic. The painter ardently seeks to create the
pure painting, the musician pure music, and someone even
told me pure radio represents the synthesis between Dionysus and Logos. Even more remarkable for our time,
not otherwise renowned for its purity, is that each and
everyone believes he has found his unique and the only
true purity. Each vestal of the arts has, if you think of
it, her own kind of chastity. Likewise, too numerous to
count, are all the theories of the theatre, of what is pure
theatre, pure tragedy, pure comedy. There are so many
modern theories of the drama, what with each playwright
keeping three or four at hand, that for this reason, if no
other, I am a bit embarrassed to come along now with
my theories of the problems of the theatre.

Furthermore, I would ask you not to look upon me as
the spokesman of some specific movement in the theatre
or of a certain dramatic technique, nor to believe that I
knock at your door as the traveling salesman of one of
the philosophies current on our stages today, whether as
existentialist, nihilist, expressionist, or satirist, or any other
label put on the compote dished up by literary criticism.
For me, the stage is not a battlefield for theories, philoso-

[1] Friedrich Duerrenmatt, "Problems of the Theatre," translated by Gerhard Nellhaus, *Tulane Drama Review*, October,
1958, pp. 3–26. Copyright 1955 by Peter Schifferli, Verlags
AG. Die Arche, Zurich. Reprinted by permission of the
author's representative, Kurt Hellmer, 52 Vanderbilt Avenue,
New York 17, New York, and Gerhard Nellhaus. This version
was prepared for publication from the manuscript of a lecture
delivered by Friedrich Duerrenmatt in the fall of 1954 and
the spring of 1955 in different cities of Switzerland and West
Germany.

phies, and manifestos, but rather an instrument whose possibilities I seek to know by playing with it. Of course, in my plays there are people and they hold to some belief or philosophy—a lot of blockheads would make for a dull piece—but my plays are not for what people have to say: what is said is there because my plays deal with people, and thinking and believing and philosophizing are all, to some extent at least, a part of human behavior. The problems I face as playwright are practical, working problems, problems I face not before, but during the writing. To be quite accurate about it, these problems usually come up after the writing is done, arising out of a certain curiosity to know how I did it. So what I would like to talk about now are these problems, even though I risk disappointing the general longing for something profound and creating the impression that an amateur is talking. I haven't the faintest notion of how else I should go about it, of how not to talk about art like an amateur. Consequently I speak only to those who fall asleep listening to Heidegger.

What I am concerned with are empirical rules, the possibilities of the theatre. But since we live in an age when literary scholarship and criticism flourish, I can not quite resist the temptation of casting a few side glances at some of the theories of the art and practice of the theatre. The artist indeed has no need of scholarship. Scholarship derives laws from what exists already; otherwise it would not be scholarship. But the laws thus established have no value for the artist, even when they are true. The artist can not accept a law he has not discovered for himself. If he can not find such a law, scholarship can not help him with one it has established; and when the artist does find one, then it does not matter that the same law was also discovered by scholarship. But scholarship, thus denied, stands behind the artist like a threatening ogre, ready to leap forth whenever the artist wants to talk about art. And so it is here. To talk about problems of the theatre is to enter into competition with literary scholarship. I undertake this with some misgivings. Literary scholarship looks on the theatre as an object; for the dramatist it is never something purely objective, something separate from him. He participates in it. It is true that the playwright's activity makes drama into something objective (that is exactly his job), but he destroys the object he has created again and again, forgets it, rejects it, scorns it, reevaluates it, all in order to make room for something new. Scholarship sees only the result; the process, which led to this result, is what the playwright can not forget. What he says has to be taken with a grain of salt. What he thinks about his art changes as he creates his art; his thoughts are always subject to his mood and the moment. What alone really counts for him is what he is doing at a given moment; for its sake he can betray what he did just a little while ago. Perhaps a writer should never talk about his art, but once he starts, then it is not altogether a waste of time to listen to him. Literary scholars who have not the faintest notion of the difficulties of writing and of the hidden rocks that force the stream of art into oft unsuspected channels run the danger of merely asserting and stupidly proclaiming laws that do not exist.

Doubtless the unities of time, place, and action which Aristotle—so it was supposed for a long time—derived from Greek tragedy constitute the ideal of drama. From a logical and hence also aesthetic point of view, this thesis is incontestable, so incontestable indeed, that the question arises if it does not set up the framework once and for all within which each dramatist must work. Aristotle's three unities demand the greatest precision, the greatest economy, and the greatest simplicity in the handling of the dramatic material. The unities of time, place, and action ought to be a basic dictate put to the dramatist by literary scholarship, and the only reason scholarship does not hold the artist to them is that Aristotle's unities have not been obeyed by anyone for ages. Nor can they be obeyed, for reasons which best illustrate the relationship of the art of writing plays to the theories about that art.

The unities of time, place, and action in essence presuppose Greek tragedy. Aristotle's unities do not make Greek tragedy possible; rather, Greek tragedy allows his unities. No matter how abstract an aesthetic law may appear to be, the work of art from which it was derived is contained in that law. If I want to set about writing a dramatic action which is to unfold and run its course in the same place inside of two hours, for instance, then this action must have a history behind it, and that history is the story which took place before the stage action commenced, a story which alone makes the action on the stage possible. Thus the history behind Hamlet is, of course, the murder of his father; the drama lies in the discovery of that murder. As a rule, too, the stage action is much shorter in time than the event depicted; it often starts out right in the middle of the event, or indeed toward the end of it. Before Sophocles' tragedy could begin, Oedipus had to have killed his father and married his mother. The stage action condenses an event to the extent to which Aristotle's unities are fulfilled; the closer a playwright adheres to the three unities, the more important is the background history of the action.

It is, of course, possible to invent a history and hence a dramatic action that would seem particularly favorable for keeping to Aristotle's unities. But this brings into force the rule that the more invented a story is and the more unknown it is to the audience, the more careful must its exposition, the unfolding of the background, be. Greek tragedy was possible only because it did not have to invent its historical background, because it already possessed one. The spectators knew the myths with which each drama dealt; and because these myths were public, ready coin, part of religion, they made the feats of the Greek tragedians possible, feats never to be attained again; they made possible their abbreviations, their straightforwardness, their stichomythy and choruses, and hence also Aristotle's unities. The audience knew what the play was all about; its curiosity was not focused on the story so much as on its treatment. Aristotle's unities presupposed the general appreciation of the subject matter—a genial exception in more recent times is Kleist's *The Broken Jug*—presupposed a religious theatre based on myths. Therefore as soon as the theatre lost its religious, its mythical significance, the unities had to be reinterpreted or discarded. An audience facing an unknown story will pay more attention to the story than to its treatment, and by necessity then such a play has to be richer in detail and circumstances than one with a known action. The feats of one playwright can not be the feats of another. Each art exploits the chances offered by its time, and it is hard to imagine a time without chances. Like every other form of art, drama creates its world; but not every world can be created in the same fashion. This is the natural limitation of every aesthetic rule, no matter how self-evident such a rule may be. This does not mean that Aristotle's unities are obsolete; what was once a rule has become an exception, a case that may occur again at any time. The one-act play obeys the unities still, even though under a different condition. The plot is dominated by a situation instead of by history, and thus unity is once again achieved.

. . . the task of art, insofar as art can have a task at all, and hence also the task of drama today, is to create something concrete, something that has form. This can be accomplished best by comedy. Tragedy, the strictest genre in art, presupposes a formed world. Comedy—insofar as it is not just satire of a particular society as in Molière —supposes an unformed world, a world being made and turned upside down, a world about to fold like ours. Tragedy overcomes distance; it can make myths originating in times immemorial seem like the present to the Athenians. But comedy creates distance; the attempt of the Athenians to gain a foothold in Sicily is translated by comedy into the birds undertaking to create their own empire before which the gods and men will have to capitulate. How comedy works can be seen in the most primitive kind of joke, in the dirty story, which, though it is of very dubious value, I bring up only because it is the best illustration of what I mean by creating distance. The subject of the dirty story is the purely sexual, and, because it is purely sexual, it is formless and without objective distance. To achieve form the purely sexual is transmuted, as I have already mentioned, into the dirty joke. Therefore this type of joke is a kind of original comedy, a transposition of the sexual onto the plain of the comical. In this way it is possible today in a society dominated by John Doe, to talk in an accepted way about the purely sexual. Thus the dirty story demonstrates that the comical exists in forming what is formless, in creating order out of chaos.

The means by which comedy creates distance is the conceit. Tragedy is without conceit. Hence there are few tragedies whose subjects were invented. By this I do not mean to imply that the ancient tragedians lacked inventive ideas of the sort that are written today, but the marvel of their art was that they had no need of these inventions, of conceits. That makes all the difference. Aristophanes, on the other hand, lives by conceits. The stuff of his plays are not myths but inventions, which take place not in the past but the present. They drop into their world like bombshells which, by poking holes into the landscape, change the present into the comic and thus scatter the dirt for everyone to see. This, of course, does not mean that drama today can only be comical. Tragedy and comedy are but formal concepts, dramatic attitudes, figments of the aesthetic imagination which can embrace one and the same thing. Only the conditions under which each is created are different, and these conditions have their basis only in small part in art.

Tragedy presupposes guilt, despair, moderation, lucidity, vision, a sense of responsibility. In the Punch-and-Judy show of our century, in this backsliding of the white race, guilty and, hence, responsible men no longer exist. On all sides we hear: "We couldn't help it," "We didn't really want that to happen." And indeed, things happen without anyone in particular being responsible for them. Everything is swept along and everyone gets caught up somehow in the current of events. We are all collectively guilty, collectively bogged down in the sins of our fathers and of our forefathers. We are the offspring of children. That is our misfortune, but not our guilt; guilt can exist only as a personal achievement, as a religious deed. What is right for us is comedy. Our world has led to the grotesque as well as to the atom bomb, and Jeronimo's madness is with us again, the apocalyptic vision has become the grotesquely real. But the grotesque is only a way of expressing in a tangible manner, of making us perceive physically the paradoxical, the form of the unformed, the face of a world without face; and just as in our thinking today we seem to be unable to do without the concept of the paradox, so also in art, and in our world which at times seems still to exist only because the atom bomb exists: out of fear of the bomb.

But the tragic is still possible even if pure tragedy is not. We can achieve the tragic out of comedy. We can bring it forth as a frightening moment, as an abyss that opens suddenly; indeed many of Shakespeare's tragedies are already really comedies out of which the tragic arises.

All this then might easily lead to the conclusion that

comedy is the expression of despair, but this conclusion is not inevitable. To be sure, whoever realizes the senselessness, the hopelessness of this world might well despair, but this despair is not a result of this world. Rather it is an answer given by an individual to this world; another answer would be not to despair, would be an individual's decision to endure this world in which we live like Gulliver among the giants. He also achieves distance, he also steps back a pace or two who takes measure of his opponent, who prepares himself to fight his opponent or to escape him. It is still possible to show man as a courageous being.

In truth this is a principal concern of mine. The blind men, Romulus, Uebelohe, Akki, are all men of courage. The lost world order is restored within them; the universal escapes my grasp. I refuse to find the universal in a doctrine. The universal for me is chaos. The world (hence the stage which represents this world) is for me something monstrous, a riddle of misfortunes which must be accepted but before which one must not capitulate. The world is far bigger than any man, and perforce threatens him constantly. If one could but stand outside the world, it would no longer be threatening. But I have neither the right nor the ability to be an outsider to this world. To find solace in poetry can also be all too cheap; it is more honest to retain one's human point of view. Brecht's thesis, that the world is an accident, which he developed in "Die Strassenszene"[2] where he shows how this accident happened, may yield—as it in fact did—some magnificent theatre; but he did it by concealing most of the evidence! Brecht's thinking is inexorable, because inexorably there are many things he will not think about.

And lastly it is through the conceit, through comedy that the anonymous audience becomes possible as an audience, becomes a reality to be counted on, and, also, one to be taken into account. The conceit easily transforms the crowd of theatregoers into a mass which can be attacked, deceived, outsmarted into listening to things it would otherwise not so readily listen to. Comedy is a mousetrap in which the public is easily caught and in which it will get caught over and over again. Tragedy, on

[2] An article from *Schriften Zum Theater,* available in an English translation by Eric Bentley under the title "A Model for Epic Theatre."

the other hand, predicates a true community, a kind of community whose existence in our day is but an embarrassing fiction. Nothing is more ludicrous, for instance, than to sit and watch the mystery plays of the Anthroposophists when one is not a participant.

Granting all this, there is still one more question to be asked: is it permissible to go from a generality to a particular form of art, to do what I just did when I went from my assertion that the world was formless to the particular possibility for writing comedies today? I doubt that this is permissible. Art is something personal, and something personal should never be explained in generalities. The value of a work of art does not depend on whether more or less good reasons for its existence can be found. Hence I have also tried to avoid certain problems, as, for example, the argument which is very lively today, whether or not plays ought to be written in verse or in prose. My own answer lies simply in writing prose, without any intentions of thereby deciding the issue. A man has to choose to go one way, after all, and why should one way always be worse than another? As far as my concepts of comedy are concerned, I believe that here, too, personal reasons are more important than more general ones that are always open to argument. What logic in matters of art could not be refuted! One talks best about art when one talks of one's own art. The art one chooses is an expression of freedom without which no art can exist, and at the same time also of necessity without which art can not exist either. The artist always represents his world and himself. If at one time philosophy taught men to arrive at the particular from the general, then unlike Schiller, who started out believing in general conclusions, I can not construct a play as he did when I doubt that the particular can ever be reached from the general. But my doubt is mine and only mine, and not the doubt and problems of a Catholic for whom drama holds possibilities non-Catholics do not share. This is so even if, on the other hand, a Catholic who takes his religion seriously, is denied those possibilities which other men possess. The danger inherent in this thesis lies in the fact that there are always those artists who for the sake of finding some generalities to believe in accept conversion, taking a step which is the more to be wondered at for the sad fact that it really will not help them. The difficulties experienced by a Protestant in writing a drama are just the same difficulties he has with his faith. Thus it is my way to mistrust what is ordinarily called the building of the drama, and to arrive at my plays from the unique, the sudden idea or conceit, rather than from some general concept or plan. Speaking for myself, I need to write off into the blue, as I like to put it so that I might give critics a catchword to hang onto. They use it often enough, too, without really understanding what I mean by it.

But these matters are my own concerns and hence it is not necessary to invoke the whole world and to make out as if what are my concerns are the concerns of art in general (lest I be like the drunk who goes back to Noah, the Flood, original sin, and the beginning of the world to explain what is, after all, only his own weakness). As in everything and everywhere, and not just in the field of art, the rule is: No excuses, please! . . .

JOHN OSBORNE
(b. 1929)

Declaration[1] (1958)

WHENEVER I sit down to write, it is always with dread in my heart. But never more than when I am about to write straightforward prose, because I know then that my failure will be greater and more obvious. There will be no exhilarating skirmishes, no small victories on the way to defeat. When I am writing for the theatre I know these small victories: when the light on my desk is too bright and my back aches, but I go on writing because I am afraid that my pen will lose the words that come into my head; when I watch an actor on an empty stage deliver something that proves to me that my sense of timing has been exact, after all. Timing is an artistic problem, it is the prime theatrical problem. You can learn it, but it cannot be taught. It must be felt. Things like this—composition, sonata form, the line that is unalterable—there are small victories to be won from them, because these are things that seem worth doing for themselves. If you are any good at all at what you set out to do, you know whether it is good and rely on no one to tell you so. You depend on no one.

It is not true to say that a play does not "come alive" until it is actually in performance. Of course it comes alive—to the man who has written it, just as those three symphonies must have come alive to Mozart during those last six weeks. One is sure to fail, but there are usually enough perks to be picked up on the way to make it bearable. It is the pattern of life itself, and it is acceptable. But whenever I sit down to write in prose about my present feelings and attitudes, my dread is enormous be-

[1] John Osborne, "They Call it Cricket," *Declaration*, edited by Tom Maschler (New York: E. P. Dutton, 1958), pp. 45–66. Copyright 1957 by MacGibbon and Kee. Reprinted by permission of E. P. Dutton and Co., Inc., and MacGibbon and Kee, London.

cause I know that there will be no perks to pick up, or if there are, that they will be negligible. . . .

Part of my job is to try and keep people interested in their seats for about two and a half hours; it is a very difficult thing to do, and I am proud of having been even fairly successful at it. *Look Back in Anger* has been playing to large audiences all over the country for months, at a time when touring is all but finished. Provincial audiences (who, on the whole, are far more receptive than West End audiences) don't remember what the posh papers said about plays, even if they read them. They go to the theatre because the guvnor's wife went on Monday night and said it was a jolly good show. I simply want to point out that my job has not been an easy one to learn, merely because I have had what looks like an easy success. I shall go on learning as long as there is a theatre standing in England, but I didn't learn the job from the *Daily Mail* or the *Spectator*.

I want to make people feel, to give them lessons in feeling. They can think afterward. In some countries this could be a dangerous approach, but there seems little danger of people feeling too much—at least not in England as I am writing. I am an artist—whether or not I am a good one is beside the point now. For the first time in my life I have a chance to get on with my job, and that is what I intend to do. I shall do it in the theatre and, possibly, in films. I shall not try and hand out my gospel version of the Labour party's next manifesto to prop up any journalist who wants a bit of easy copy or to give some reviewer another smart clue for his weekly written-up crossword game. I shall simply fling down a few statements—you can take your pick. They will be what are often called "sweeping statements" but I believe we are living at a time when a few "sweeping statements" may be valuable. It is too late for caution.

When my play *The Entertainer* was produced, it was complained that one of the characters was "vaguely anti-queen." Now if this character was vague in the way she expressed herself, it was because the existence of the Lord Chamberlain's office compelled it. I should have been delighted if she could have been more explicit, although, in this case, I was anxious that this particular point should not be made too literally. The bigger point that this character was trying to make was something like: "What kind of symbols do we live by? *Are* they truthful and worthwhile?" But in expressing herself in anti-queen terms, which was a relevant and colorful image—or so I thought—I believe she was asking an important question. I still believe it to be an important question.

Recently I read an article by David Marquand called *"Lucky Jim* and the Labour Party." . . . The principal figures seem to have been Kingsley Amis, John Wain —and myself. A great deal of the *Lucky Jim* gibberish has been promoted by a few words I put into the mouth of Jimmy Porter [*Look Back in Anger*]. These were: "There aren't any good, brave causes left." Immediately they heard this, all the shallow heads with their savage thirst for trimmed-off explanations got to work on it, and they had enough new symbols to play about with happily and fill their columns for half a year. They believed him, just as some believed Archie Rice [*The Entertainer*] when he said, "I don't feel a thing" or "I may be an old pouf, but I'm not right-wing." They were incapable of recognizing the texture of ordinary despair, the way it expresses itself in rhetoric and gestures that may perhaps look shabby, but are seldom simple. It is too simple to say that Jimmy Porter himself believed that there were no good, brave causes left, any more than Archie didn't feel a thing.

At this I can hear all kinds of impatient inflections. "Well, if your characters only mean what they say some of the time, when are we supposed to know what they're getting at? What are *you* getting at? What do you *mean?* How do you *explain* these characters, these situations?" At every performance of any of my plays, there are always some of these deluded pedants, sitting there impatiently, waiting for the plugs to come singing in during natural breaks in the action. If the texture is too complex, they complain that too much is going on for them to follow. There they sit, these fashionable turnips, the death's heads of imagination and feeling, longing for the interval and its overprojected drawls of ignorance. Like the B.B.C. critics, they either have no ear at all, or they can never listen to themselves.

I offer no explanations to such people. All art is organized evasion. You respond to Lear or Max Miller— or you don't. I can't teach the paralyzed to move their limbs. Shakespeare didn't describe symptoms or offer explanations. Neither did Chekhov. Neither do I.

It is an inescapable fact that when the middle classes discuss experience that is not dominated by their own emotional values, they hedge and bluster with all they've got. A few weeks ago, a reviewer wrote: "One is compelled to believe that if they [the characters] have indeed been drawn from life, Mr. Osborne has set them down with shamelessly pointed accuracy." This, at least, is refreshingly honest. There is no pretense at being capable of judging whether the characters have been indeed drawn from life—just a shrug at shamelessly pointed accuracy. The boys in the orchestra at the Royal Court Theatre were capable of judging, and they did: *"We've been through it and we know what it is like."* This is what audiences have muttered beneath their heartbeat as they have watched Oedipus or Lear or Willy Loman. "It's still a bitter truth of life," says the same writer, "that the most wretched human beings become bores when they start moaning—even the sick, the aged, and afflicted." This sentence sums up fairly neatly a prevalent class attitude to the pain and struggle of other people. I do not accept it for one moment. It is true that the middle classes do not talk about their private troubles. But like working people they do moan a great deal about the way they think they are being cheated out of their inheritance, submerged by taxes and unfair checks on their "incentive"—in other words they are not allowed to make enough money to buy themselves their traditional privileges—the education that will assure them of the best places in the sun. But, on the whole, they scrupulously avoid discussing their personal problems. Even with their friends.

I am not going to define my own socialism. Socialism is an experimental idea, not a dogma; an attitude to truth and liberty, the way people should live and treat each other. Individual definitions are unimportant. The difference between socialist and Tory values should have been made clear enough by this time. I am a writer and my own contribution to a socialist society is to demonstrate those values in my own medium, not to discover the best ways of implementing them. I don't need to step outside my own home to canvass for the Labour party. Years ago, T.S.

Eliot wrote: "In a society like ours, worm-eaten with Liberalism, the only thing possible for a person with strong convictions is to state a point of view and leave it at that." Substitute Toryism for Liberalism, and I'd say that this very roughly sums up my present socialist attitude—an experimental attitude to feeling. All the fields of experiment must be tackled by their own experts—economists and sociologists, town planners and educationists, industrial psychologists, observers, lawmakers, and truth seekers.

Nobody can be very interested in my contribution to a problem like the kind of houses people should have built for them, the kind of school they should send their children to, or the pensions they should be able to look forward to. But there are other questions to be asked—how do people live inside those houses? What is their relationship with one another, and with their children, with their neighbors and the people across the street, or on the floor above? What are the things that are important to them, that make them care, give them hope and anxiety? What kind of language do they use to one another? What is the meaning of the work they do? Where does the pain lie? What are their expectations? What moves them, brings them together, makes them speak out? Where is the weakness, the loneliness? Where are the things that are unrealized? Where is the strength? Experiment means asking questions, and these are all the questions of socialism.

EUGENE IONESCO
(b. 1912)

The Starting Point[1] (1955)

ALL MY PLAYS have their origin in two fundamental states
of consciousness: now the one, now the other is predom-
inant, and sometimes they are combined. These basic
states of consciousness are an awareness of evanescence
and of solidity, of emptiness and of too much presence,
of the unreal transparency of the world and its opacity,
of light and of thick darkness. Each of us has surely
felt at moments that the substance of the world is dreamlike, that the walls are no longer solid, that we seem to
be able to see through everything into a spaceless universe made up of pure light and color; at such a moment
the whole of life, the whole history of the world, becomes
useless, senseless, and impossible. When you fail to go
beyond this first stage of *dépaysement*—for you really
do have the impression you are waking to a world unknown
—the sensation of evanescence gives you a feeling of
anguish, a form of giddiness. But all this may equally
well lead to euphoria: the anguish suddenly turns into release; nothing counts now except the wonder of being, that
new and amazing consciousness of life in the glow of a
fresh dawn, when we have found our freedom again; the
fact of being astonishes us, in a world that now seems all
illusion and pretense, in which all human behavior tells of
absurdity and all history of absolute futility; all reality
and all language appear to lose their articulation, to dis-
integrate and collapse, so what possible reaction is there
left, when everything has ceased to matter, but to laugh
at it all? I myself at one such moment felt so completely
free, so released, that I had the impression I could do
anything I wished with the language and the people of a

[1] Eugene Ionesco, Foreword, *Plays*, translated by Donald
Watson (London: John Calder, 1959), I, vii–ix. Reprinted by
courtesy of Eugene Ionesco and Donald Watson.

world that no longer seemed to me anything but a base-
less and ridiculous sham.

Of course this state of consciousness is very rare; this
joy and wonder at being alive, in a universe that troubles
me no more and *is* no more, can only just hold; more
commonly the opposite feeling prevails: what is light grows
heavy, the transparent becomes dense, the world op-
presses, the universe is crushing me. A curtain, an impassable wall stands between me and the world, between
me and myself; matter fills every corner, takes up all the
space and its weight annihilates all freedom; the horizon
closes in and the world becomes a stifling dungeon.
Language breaks down in a different way and words drop
like stones or dead bodies; I feel I am invaded by heavy
forces, against which I can only fight a losing battle.

This was definitely the starting point of those of my
plays that are generally considered the more dramatic:
Amédée and *Victims of Duty.* Given such a state of
mind, words, their magic gone, are obviously replaced by
objects, by properties: countless mushrooms sprout in
the flat of Amédée and Madeleine; a dead body suffering from "geometrical progression" grows there too and
turns the tenants out; in *Victims of Duty,* when coffee is
to be served to three of the characters, there is a
mounting pile of hundreds of cups; the furniture in *The
New Tenant* first blocks up every staircase in the building,
then clutters the stage, and finally entombs the character
who came to take a room in the house; in *The Chairs*
the stage is filled with dozens of chairs for invisible guests;
and in *Jacques* several noses appear on the face of a
young girl. When words are worn out, the mind is worn
out. The universe, encumbered with matter, is then empty
of presence: "too much" links up with "not enough"
and objects are the materialization of solitude, of the
victory of the anti-spiritual forces, of everything we are
struggling against. But in this anxious situation I do
not quite give up the fight, and if, as I hope, I manage in
spite of the anguish to introduce into the anguish, humor
—which is a happy symptom of the other presence—this
humor is my outlet, my release, and my salvation.

I have no intention of passing judgment on my plays.
It is not for me to do so. I have simply tried to give
some indication of what emotional material went into their
making, of what was at their source: a mood and not an

ideology, an impulse not a program; the cohesive unity that grants formal structure to emotions in their primitive state satisfies an inner need and does not answer the logic of some structural order imposed from without; not submission to some predetermined action, but the exteriorization of a psychic dynamism, a projection onto the stage of internal conflict, of the universe that lies within: but as the microcosm is in the likeness of the macrocosm and each one of us is all the others, it is in the deepest part of myself, of my anguish and my dreams, it is in my solitude that I have the best chance of rediscovering the universal, the common ground.

The Bald Soprano is the only one of my plays the critics consider to be "purely comic." And yet there again the comic seems to me to be an expression of the unusual. But in my view the unusual can spring only from the dullest and most ordinary daily routine and from our everyday prose, when pursued beyond their limits. To feel the absurdity, the improbability of everyday experience and of our attempts at communication is already to have gone a stage further; before you do this, you must first saturate yourself. The comic is the unusual pure and simple; nothing surprises me more than banality; the "surreal" is there, within our reach, in our daily conversation.

PART 2 Creations

A Doll's House[1] (1878)

NOTES FOR THE MODERN TRAGEDY

THERE ARE two kinds of spiritual law, two kinds of conscience, one in man and another, altogether different, in woman. They do not understand each other; but in practical life the woman is judged by man's law, as though she were not a woman but a man.

The wife in the play ends by having no idea of what is right or wrong; natural feeling on the one hand and belief in authority on the other have altogether bewildered her.

A woman cannot be herself in the society of the present day, which is an exclusively masculine society, with laws framed by men and with a judicial system that judges feminine conduct from a masculine point of view.

She has committed forgery, and she is proud of it; for she did it out of love for her husband, to save his life. But this husband with his commonplace principles of

---

[1] Henrik Ibsen, *From Ibsen's Workshop,* translated by A. G. Chater, *The Works of Henrik Ibsen.* (New York: Charles Scribner's Sons, 1912), XII, pp. 91–95 (*A Doll's House*), pp. 185–86 (*Ghosts*). "This volume contains all the notes, sketches, drafts, and other 'foreworks' (as he used to call them) for Ibsen's plays from *Pillars of Society* onwards. . . . The papers here translated throw invaluable light upon the genesis of his ideas and the development of his technique. They are an indispensable aid to the study of his intellectual processes during that part of his career which made him world famous. . . . Nowhere else, so far as I am aware, do we obtain so clear a view of the processes of a great dramatist's mind" (from the introduction by William Archer). "Of *A Doll's House* we possess a first brief memorandum, a fairly detailed scenario, a complete draft, in quite actable form, and a few detached fragments of dialogue" (Archer).

honor is on the side of the law and looks at the question from the masculine point of view.

Spiritual conflicts. Oppressed and bewildered by the belief in authority, she loses faith in her moral right and ability to bring up her children. Bitterness. A mother in modern society, like certain insects who go away and die when she has done her duty in the propagation of the race. Love of life, of home, of husband and children and family. Now and then a womanly shaking off of her thoughts. Sudden return of anxiety and terror. She must bear it all alone. The catastrophe approaches, inexorably, inevitably. Despair, conflict, and destruction.

(Krogstad has acted dishonorably and thereby become well-to-to-do; now his prosperity does not help him, he cannot recover his honor.)

SCENARIO: FIRST ACT

A room comfortably, but not showily, furnished. A door to the right in the back leads to the hall; another door to the left in the back leads to the room or office of the master of the house, which can be seen when the door is opened. A fire in the stove. Winter day.

She enters from the back, humming gaily; she is in outdoor dress and carries several parcels, has been shopping. As she opens the door, a porter is seen in the hall, carrying a Christmas tree. She: Put it down there for the present. (Taking out her purse) How much? Porter: Fifty öre. She: Here is a crown. No, keep the change. The porter thanks her and goes. She continues humming and smiling contentedly as she opens several of the parcels she has brought. Calls off to find out if he is home. Yes! At first, conversation through the closed door; then he opens it and goes on talking to her while continuing to work most of the time, standing at his desk. There is a ring at the hall door; he does not want to be disturbed; shuts himself in. The maid opens the door to her mistress's friend, just arrived in town. Happy surprise. Mutual explanation of the state of affairs. He has received the post of manager in the new joint-stock bank and is to begin at New Year's; all financial worries are at an end. The friend has come to town to look for some small employment in an office or whatever may present itself. Mrs. Stenborg encourages her, is certain that all will turn

out well. The maid opens the front door to the debt
collector. Mrs. Stenborg terrified; they exchange a few
words; he is shown into the office. Mrs. Stenborg and her
friend; the circumstances of the collector are touched
upon. Stenborg enters in his overcoat; has sent the collector out the other way. Conversation about the friend's
affairs; hesitation on his part. He and the friend go out;
his wife follows them into the hall; the Nurse enters with
the children. Mother and children play. The collector
enters. Mrs. Stenborg sends the children out to the left.
Big scene between her and him. He goes. Stenborg enters;
has met him on the stairs; displeased; wants to know what
he came back for? Her support? No intrigues. His wife
cautiously tries to pump him. Strict legal answers. Exit
to his room. *She:* (repeating her words when the collector
went out) But that's impossible. Why, I did it from love!

SECOND ACT

The last day of the year. Midday. Nora and the old
Nurse. Nora, driven by anxiety, is putting on her things
to go out. Anxious random questions of one kind and
another intimate that thoughts of death are in her mind.
Tries to banish these thoughts, to make light of it, hopes
that something or other may intervene. But what? The
Nurse goes off to the left. Stenborg enters from his room.
Short dialogue between him and Nora. The Nurse re-enters;
looks for Nora; the youngest child is crying. Annoyance
and questioning on Stenborg's part; exit the Nurse;
Stenborg is going in to the children. Doctor enters.
Scene between him and Stenborg. Nora soon re-enters;
she has turned back; anxiety has driven her home again.
Scene between her, the Doctor, and Stenborg. Stenborg
goes into his room. Scene between Nora and the Doctor.
The Doctor goes out. Nora alone. Mrs. Linde enters.
Scene between her and Nora. Lawyer Krogstad enters.
Short scene between him, Mrs. Linde, and Nora. Mrs.
Linde in to the children. Scene between Krogstad and
Nora. She entreats and implores him for the sake of her
little children; in vain. Krogstad goes out. The letter is
seen to fall from outside into the letter box. Mrs. Linde
re-enters after a short pause. Scene between her and
Nora. Half confession. Mrs. Linde goes out. Nora alone.
Stenborg enters. Scene between him and Nora. He wants

to empty the letter box. Entreaties, jests, half-playful persuasion. He promises to let business wait till after New Year's Day; but at 12 o'clock midnight . . . ! Exit. Nora alone. *Nora:* (looking at the clock) It is five o'clock. Five; seven hours till midnight. Twenty-four hours till the next midnight. Twenty-four and seven—thirty-one. Thirty-one hours to live.

THIRD ACT

A muffled sound of dance music is heard from the floor above. A lighted lamp on the table. Mrs. Linde sits in an armchair and absently turns the pages of a book, tries to read, but seems unable to fix her attention; once or twice she looks at her watch. Nora comes down from the party; so disturbed she was compelled to leave; surprise at finding Mrs. Linde, who pretends that she wanted to see Nora in her costume. Helmer, displeased at her going away, comes to fetch her back. The Doctor also enters, to say good-by. Meanwhile Mrs. Linde has gone into the side room on the right. Scene between the Doctor, Helmer, and Nora. He is going to bed, he says, never to get up again; they are not to come and see him; there is ugliness about a deathbed. He goes out. Helmer goes upstairs again with Nora, after the latter has exchanged a few words of farewell with Mrs. Linde. Mrs. Linde alone. Then Krogstad. Scene and explanation between them. Both go out. Nora and the children. Then she alone. Then Helmer. He takes the letters out of the letter box. Short scene; good night; he goes into his room. Nora in despair prepares for the final step, is already at the door when Helmer enters with the open letter in his hand. Big scene. A ring. Letter to Nora from Krogstad. Final scene. Divorce. Nora leaves the house.

Ghosts[2]

THE PLAY is to be like a picture of life. Belief undermined. But it does not do to say so. "The Orphanage"—

[2] "Of the studies for *Ghosts* only a few brief fragments have been preserved. The most important of these are mere casual memoranda, some of them written on the back of an envelope

for the sake of others. They are to be happy—but this too is only an appearance—everything is ghosts.

A leading point: She has been a believer and romantic —this is not entirely obliterated by the standpoint reached later—"Everything is ghosts."

Marriage for external reasons, even when these are religious or moral, brings a Nemesis upon the offspring.

She, the illegitimate child, can be saved by being married to—the son—but then—?

¶ He was dissipated and his health was shattered in his youth; then she appeared, the religious enthusiast; she saved him; she was rich. He was going to marry a girl who was considered unworthy. He had a son by his wife, then he went back to the girl; a daughter.

¶ These modern women, ill-used as daughters, as sisters, as wives, not educated according to their gifts, prevented from following their calling, deprived of their inheritance, embittered in temper—it is these who furnish the mothers of the new generation. What will be the result?

¶ The keynote is to be: The prolific growth of our intellectual life, in literature, arts, etc.—and in contrast to this: all of mankind gone astray.

The complete human being is no longer a product of nature, he is an artificial product like grain, and fruit trees, and the Creole race and thoroughbred horses and dogs, the vine, etc.

The fault lies in that all mankind has failed. If a man claims to live and develop in a human way, it is megalomania. All mankind, and especially the Christian part of it, suffers from megalomania.

¶ Among us, monuments are erected to the *dead,* since we have a duty toward them; we allow lepers to marry; but their offspring . . . ? The unborn . . . ?

---

addressed to 'Madame Ibsen.' These memoranda fall into six sections, of which the fourth and fifth seem to have as much bearing on other plays—for instance, on *An Enemy of the People* and *The Lady From the Sea* as on *Ghosts.* I should take them rather for detached jottings than for notes specially referring to that play" (Archer).

Hedda Gabler[3]

(1)

¶ This married woman more and more imagines that she is an important personality, and as a consequence feels compelled to create for herself a sensational past—

¶ If an interesting female character appears in a new story or in a play, she believes that it is she who is being portrayed.

¶ The masculine environment helps to confirm her in this belief.

¶ The two lady friends agree to die together. One of them carries out her end of the bargain. But the other one who realizes what lies in store for her loses her courage. This is the reversal—

---

[3] More preliminary notes have been preserved for *Hedda Gabler* than for almost any other play by Ibsen. These notes afford the student of playwriting a rare opportunity to trace the growth of a masterpiece from the first embryonic thoughts through its birth as a full-length draft. Nearly all of these preliminary notes are given here, grouped in seven sets to indicate their different sources: scattered loose sheets, notebooks, even a calling card. Of greatest interest are the notes in sets 1 and 5 taken from a little black book, now in the possession of Tancred Ibsen, which Ibsen carried about with him. According to Else Høst, *Hedda Gabler: En monografi* (Oslo: 1958), pp. 78 ff., the notes in set 1 were probably jotted down in the fall of 1889 and comprise the abortive ideas for a play about a prominent woman novelist, Camilla Collett, who imagined that Ibsen had used her as a model for the heroine of *The Lady from the Sea*. Ibsen made no progress with this play, but among the notes for it he had planted the seeds of another play: a play about a cowardly woman, the woman's jealousy of a man with a mission in life, and a misplaced manuscript which represents that mission. The lengthy sequence of notes in set 5, almost certainly in chronological order, was probably made during the winter and spring of 1890 and reveals the convolutions of Ibsen's thought as the characters, plot, and motives of *Hedda Gabler* take shape. In late July or early August, Ibsen began to write a full-length draft, most of which is translated in *From Ibsen's Workshop*, Vol. XII of the Archer edition of Ibsen's Collected Works. This draft was thoroughly revised in October, fair copied in October and November, and *Hedda Gabler* was published on December 4, 1890, in time for the Christmas season. The notes are arranged in the order given in the Centennial Edition of Ibsen's works (21 vols.; Oslo: 1928–1957), ed. Francis Bull, Halvdan Koht, and Didrik Arup Seip, XI, pp. 496–516. (Translator's note.)

¶ "He has such a disgusting way of walking when one sees him from behind."

¶ She hates him because he has a goal, a mission in life. The lady friend has one too, but does not dare to devote herself to it. Her personal life treated in fictional form.

¶ In the second act the manuscript that is left behind—

¶ "The lost soul" apologizes for the man of culture. The wild horse and the race horse. Drinks—eats paprika. House and clothes. Revolution against the laws of nature —but nothing stupid, not until the position is secure.

(2)

¶ The pale, apparently cold beauty. Expects great things of life and the joy of life.

The man who has now finally won her, plain and simple in appearance, but an honest and talented, broad-minded scholar.

(3)

¶ The manuscript that H. L. leaves behind contends that man's mission is: Upward, toward the bearer of light. Life on the present foundations of society is not worth living. Therefore he escapes from it through his imagination. By drinking, etc.—Tesman stands for correct behavior. Hedda for blasé oversophistication. Mrs. R. is the nervous-hysterical modern individual. Brack represents the personal bourgeois point of view.

¶ Then H. departs this world. And the two of them are left sitting there with the manuscript they cannot interpret. And the aunt is with them. What an ironic comment on humanity's striving for progress and development.

¶ But Holger's double nature intervenes. Only by realizing the basely bourgeois can he win a hearing for his great central idea.

¶ Mrs. Rising is afraid that H., although "a model of propriety," is not normal. She can only guess at his way of thinking but cannot understand it. Quotes some of his remarks—

¶ One talks about building railways and highways for the cause of progress. But no, no, that is not what is needed. Space must be cleared so that the spirit of

man can make its great turnabout. For it has gone astray.
The spirit of man has gone astray.

¶ *Holger:* I have been out. I have behaved obscenely.
That doesn't matter. But the police know about it.
That's what counts.

¶ H. L.'s despair lies in that he wants to master the
world but cannot master himself.

¶ Tesman believes that it is he who has in a way
seduced H. L. into indulging in excesses again. But that
is not so. It is as Hedda has said: that it was *he* she
dreamed of when she talked about "the famous man."
But she does not dare tell Tesman this.

¶ To aid in understanding his own character, L. has
made notes in "the manuscript." These are the notes
the two of them should interpret, want to interpret, but
cannot possibly.

¶ Brack is inclined to live as a bachelor, and then
gain admittance to a good home, become a friend of
the family, indispensable—

¶ They say it is a law of nature. Very well then, raise
an opposition to it. Demand its repeal. Why give way.
Why surrender unconditionally—

¶ In conversations between T. and L. the latter says that
he lives for his studies. The former replies that in
that case he can compete with him.—(T. lives *on* his
studies) that's the point.

¶ L. (Tesman) says: I couldn't step on a worm! "But
now I can tell you that I too am seeking the professorship. We are rivals."

(4)

¶ She has respect for his knowledge, an eye for his
noble character, but is embarrassed by his insignificant,
ridiculous appearance, makes fun of his conduct and
remarks.

(5)

¶ The aunt asks all sorts of ambiguous questions to
find out about those things that arouse her imagination
the most.

¶ NOTES: One evening as Hedda and Tesman, together with some others, were on their way home from a

party, Hedda remarked as they walked by a charming house that was where she would like to live. She meant it, but she said it only to keep the conversation with Tesman going. "He simply cannot carry on a conversation."

The house was actually for rent or sale. Tesman had been pointed out as the coming young man. And later when he proposed, and let slip that he too had dreamed of living there, she accepted.

He too had liked the house very much.

They get married. And they rent the house.[4]

But when Hedda returns as a young wife, with a vague sense of responsibility, the whole thing seems distasteful to her. She conceives a kind of hatred for the house just because it has become her home. She confides this to Brack. She evades the question with Tesman.

¶ The play shall deal with "the impossible," that is, to aspire to and strive for something which is against all the conventions, against that which is acceptable to conscious minds—Hedda's included.

¶ The episode of the hat makes Aunt Rising lose her composure. She leaves—That it could be taken for the maid's hat—no, that's going too far!

That my hat, which I've had for over nine years, could be taken for the maid's—no, that's really too much!

¶ *Hedda:* Yes, once I thought it must be wonderful to live here and own this house.

Brack: But now you are contradicting yourself.

Hedda: That may be so. But that's how it is anyway.

¶ *Hedda:* I don't understand these self-sacrificing people. Look at old Miss Rising. She has a paralyzed sister in her house, who has been lying in bed for years. Do you suppose she thinks it is a sacrifice to live for that poor creature, who is a burden even to herself? Far from it! Just the opposite. I don't understand it.

¶ *Hedda:* And how greedy they are for married

---

[4] Both of them, each in his and her own way, have seen in their common love for this house a sign of their mutual understanding. As if they sought and were drawn to a common home.

Then he rents the house. They get married and go abroad. He orders the house bought and his aunt furnishes it at his expense. Now it is their home. It is theirs and yet it is not, because it is not paid for. Everything depends on his getting the professorship. (Ibsen's note.)

men. Do you know what, Judge Brack? You don't do
yourself any good by not getting married.

Brack: Then I can practically consider myself married.

Hedda: Yes, you certainly can—in one way—in
many ways even—

Brack: In many ways? What do you mean by that?

Hedda: No thanks. I won't tell you.

¶ When Mrs. Elvsted says that the first part of
Lövborg's book deals with the historical development of
"Sociology," and that another volume will appear later,
Tesman looks at her a little startled.

¶ Very few true parents are to be found in the world.
Most people grow up under the influence of aunts or
uncles—either neglected and misunderstood or else spoiled.

¶ Hedda rejects him because he does not dare expose
himself to temptation. He replies that the same is true
of her. The wager! . . . He loses . . . ! Mrs. Elvsted is
present. Hedda says: No danger—He loses.

¶ Hedda feels herself demoniacally attracted by
the tendencies of the times. But she lacks courage. Her
thoughts remain theories, ineffective dreams.[5]

¶ The feminine imagination is not active and inde-
pendently creative like the masculine. It needs a bit of
reality as a help.

¶ Lövborg has had inclinations toward "the bohemian
life." Hedda is attracted in the same direction, but she
does not dare to take the leap.

¶ Buried deep within Hedda there is a level of
poetry. But the environment frightens her. Suppose she
were to make herself ridiculous!

¶ Hedda realizes that she, much more than Thea, has
abandoned her husband.

¶ The newly wedded couple return home in September
—as the summer is dying. In the second act they sit
in the garden—but with their coats on.

¶ Being frightened by one's own voice. Something
strange, foreign.

¶ NEWEST PLAN: The festivities in Tesman's garden
—and Lövborg's defeat—already prepared for in the 1st
act. Second act: the party—

[5] This note is omitted in the Centennial Edition. It is translated from Else Høst, *Hedda Gabler: En monografi* (Oslo:
1958), p. 82.

¶ Hedda energetically refuses to serve as hostess. She will not celebrate their marriage because (in her opinion, it isn't a marriage)

¶ *Holger:* Don't you see? I am the cause of your marriage—

¶ Hedda is the type of woman in her position and with her character. She marries Tesman but she devotes her imagination to Eilert Lövborg. She leans back in her chair, closes her eyes, and dreams of his adventures. . . . This is the enormous difference: Mrs. Elvsted "works for his moral improvement." But for Hedda he is the object of cowardly, tempting daydreams. In reality she does not have the courage to be a part of anything like that. Then she realizes her condition. Caught! Can't comprehend it. Ridiculous! Ridiculous!

¶ The traditional delusion that one man and one woman are made for each other. Hedda has her roots in the conventional. She marries Tesman but she dreams of Eilert Lövborg. . . . She is disgusted by the latter's flight from life. He believes that this has raised him in her estimation. . . . Thea Elvsted is the conventional, sentimental, hysterical Philistine.

¶ Those Philistines, Mrs. E. and Tesman, explain my behavior by saying first I drink myself drunk and that the rest is done in insanity. It's a flight from reality which is an absolute necessity to me.

¶ *E. L.:* Give me something—a flower—at our parting. Hedda hands him the revolver.

Then Tesman arrives: Has he gone? "Yes." Do you think he will still compete against me? No, I don't think so. You can set your mind at rest.

¶ Tesman relates that when they were in Gratz she did not want to visit her relatives—

He misunderstands her real motives.

¶ In the last act as Tesman, Mrs. Elvsted, and Miss Rysing are consulting, Hedda plays in the small room at the back. She stops. The conversation continues. She appears in the doorway—Good night—I'm going now. Do you need me for anything? Tesman: No, nothing at all. Good night, my dear! . . . The shot is fired—

¶ CONCLUSION: All rush into the back room. Brack sinks as if paralyzed into a chair near the stove: But God have mercy—people don't *do* such things!

¶ When Hedda hints at her ideas to Brack, he says: Yes, yes, that's extraordinarily amusing—Ha ha ha! He does not understand that she is quite serious.

¶ Hedda is right in this: There is no love on Tesman's part. Nor on the aunt's part. However full of love she may be.

Eilert Lövborg has a double nature. It is a fiction that one loves only *one* person. He loves two—or many —alternately (to put it frivolously). But how can he explain his position? Mrs. Elvsted, who forces him to behave correctly, runs away from her husband. Hedda, who drives him beyond all limits, draws back at the thought of a scandal.

¶ Neither he nor Mrs. Elvsted understands the point. Tesman reads in the manuscript that was left behind about "the two ideals." Mrs. Elvsted can't explain to him what E. L. meant. Then comes the burlesque note: both T. and Mrs. E. are going to devote their future lives to interpreting the mystery.

¶ Tesman thinks that Hedda hates E. L.

Mrs. Elvsted thinks so too.

Hedda sees their delusion but dares not disabuse them of it. There is something beautiful about having an aim in life. Even if it is a delusion —

She cannot do it. Take part in someone else's.

That is when she shoots herself.

The destroyed manuscript is entitled "The ~~Philosophy~~ Ethics of Future Society."

¶ Tesman is on the verge of losing his head. All this work meaningless. New thoughts! New visions! A whole new world! Then the two of them sit there, trying to find the meaning in it. Can't make any sense of it. . . .

¶ The greatest misery in this world is that so many have nothing to do but pursue happiness without being able to find it.

¶ "From Jochum Tesman there developed a Jørgen Tesman—but it will be a long, long time before this Jørgen gives rise to a George."

¶ The simile: The journey of life = the journey on a train.

H.: One doesn't usually jump out of the compartment.

No, not when the train is moving.

Nor stand still when it is stationary. There's always someone on the platform, staring in.

¶ *Hedda:* Dream of a scandal—yes, I understand that well enough. But commit one—no, no, no.

¶ *Lövborg:* Now I understand. My ideal was an illusion. You aren't a bit better than I. Now I have nothing left to live for. Except pleasure—dissipation—as you call it. . . Wait, here's a present (The pistol)

¶ Tesman is nearsighted. Wears glasses. My, what a beautiful rose! Then he stuck his nose in the cactus. Ever since then—!

¶ NB: The mutual hatred of women. Women have no influence on external matters of government. Therefore they want to have an influence on souls. And then so many of them have no aim in life (the lack thereof is inherited)—

¶ Lövborg and Hedda bent over the photographs at the table.

He: How is it possible? *She:* Why not? *L.:* Tesman! You couldn't find words enough to make fun of him. . . . Then comes the story about the general's "disgrace," dismissal, etc. The worst thing for a lady at a ball is not to be admired for her own sake. . . *L.:* And Tesman? He took you for the sake of your person. That's just as unbearable to think about.

¶ Just by marrying Tesman it seems to me I have gotten so unspeakably far away from him.

¶ *He:* Look at her. Just look at her! . . . *Hedda:* (stroking her hair) Yes, isn't she beautiful!

¶ Men and women don't belong to the same century. . . . What a great prejudice that one should love only *one!*

¶ Hedda and Brack talk about traveling to the small university towns. *Hedda:* Now I'm not counting that little trip through the Tyrol—

¶ *Brack:* (to Tesman) Are you blind and deaf? Can't you see? Can't you hear—

Tesman: Ah. Take the manuscript. Read to me!

¶ The demoniacal element in Hedda is this: She wants to exert her influence on someone—But once she has done so, she despises him. . . . The manuscript?

¶ In the third act Hedda questions Mrs. Elvsted. But if he's like that, why is he worth holding on to. . . . Yes, yes, I know—

¶ Hedda's discovery that her relations with the maid cannot possibly be proper.

¶ In his conversation with Hedda, Lövborg says: Miss
H—Miss—You know, I don't believe that you are married.

¶ *Hedda:* And now I sit here and talk with these Philis-
tines—And the way we once could talk to each other—
No, I won't say any more. . . Talk? How do you mean?
Obscenely? Ish. Let us say indecently.

¶ NB!! The reversal in the play occurs during the big
scene between Hedda and E. L. *He:* What a wretched
business it is to conform to the existing morals. It
would be ideal if a man of the present could live the life
of the future. What a miserable business it is to fight
over a professorship!

Hedda—that lovely girl! *H.:* No! *E. L.:* Yes, I'm
going to say it. That lovely, cold girl—cold as marble.

I'm not dissipated fundamentally. But the life of
reality isn't livable—

¶ In the fifth act: *Hedda:* How hugely comic it is that
those two harmless people, Tesman and Mrs. E., should
try to put the pieces together for a monument to E. L.
The man who so deeply despised the whole business—

¶ Life becomes for Hedda a ridiculous affair that isn't
"worth seeing through to the end."

¶ The happiest mission in life is to place the people
of today in the conditions of the future.

L.: Never put a child in this world, H.!

¶ When Brack speaks of a "triangular affair," Hedda
thinks about what is going to happen and refers ambigu-
ously to it. Brack doesn't understand.

¶ Brack cannot bear to be in a house where there are
small children. "Children shouldn't be allowed to exist
until they are fourteen or fifteen. That is, girls. What
about boys? Shouldn't be allowed to exist at all—or else
they should be raised outside the house."

¶ H. admits that children have always been a horror
to her too.

¶ Hedda is strongly but imprecisely opposed to the
idea that one should love "the family." The aunts mean
nothing to her.

¶ It liberated Hedda's spirit to serve as a confessor
to E. L. Her sympathy has secretly been on his side—
But it became ugly when the public found out everything.
Then she backed out.

¶ MAIN POINTS:

1. They are not all made to be mothers.
2. They are passionate but they are afraid of scandal.
3. They perceive that the times are full of missions worth devoting one's life to, but they cannot discover them.

¶ And besides Tesman is not exactly a professional, but he is a specialist. The Middle Ages are dead—

¶ T.: Now there you see also the great advantages to my studies. I can lose manuscripts and rewrite them—no inspiration needed—

¶ Hedda is completely taken up by the child that is to come, but when it is born she dreads what is to follow—

¶ Hedda must say somewhere in the play that she did not like to get out of her compartment while on the trip. Why not? I don't like to show my legs. . . . Ah, Mrs. H., but they do indeed show themselves. Nevertheless, I don't.

¶ Shot herself! Shot herself!

Brack (collapsing in the easy chair): But great God—people don't *do* such things!

¶ NB!! Eilert Lövborg believes that a comradeship must be formed between man and woman out of which the truly spiritual human being can arise. Whatever else the two of them do is of no concern. This is what the people around him do not understand. To them he is dissolute. Inwardly he is not.

¶ If a man can have several male friends, why can't he have several lady friends?

¶ It is precisely the sensual feelings that are aroused while in the company of his female "friends" or "comrades" that seek release in his excesses.

¶ Now I'm going. Don't you have some little remembrance to give me—? You have flowers—and so many other things—(The story of the pistol from before)—But you won't use it anyhow—

¶ In the fourth act when Hedda finds out that he has shot himself, she is jubilant. . . . He had courage.

Here is the rest of the manuscript.

¶ CONCLUSION: Life isn't tragic. . . . Life is ridiculous. . . . And that's what I can't bear.

¶ Do you know what happens in novels? All those who kill themselves—through the head—not in the stomach. . . . How ridiculous—how baroque—

· ¶ In her conversation with Thea in the first act, Hedda

remarks that she cannot understand how one can fall in love with an unmarried man—or an unengaged man —or an unloved man—on the other hand—[6]

¶ Brack understands well enough that it is Hedda's repression, her hysteria that motivates everything she does.

¶ On her part, Hedda suspects that Brack sees through her without believing that she understands.

¶ *H.:* It must be wonderful to take something from someone.

¶ When H. talks to B. in the fifth act about those two sitting there trying to piece together the manuscript without the spirit being present, she breaks out in laughter. . . . Then she plays the piano—then—d—

¶ Men—in the most indescribable situations how ridiculous they are.

¶ NB! She really wants to live a *man's* life wholly. But then she has misgivings. Her inheritance, what is implanted in her.

¶ Loving and being loved by aunts . . . Most people who are born of old maids, male and female.

¶ This deals with the "underground forces and powers." Woman as a minor. Nihilism. Father and mother belonging to different eras. The female underground revolution in thought. The slave's fear of the outside world.

¶ NB!! Why should I conform to social morals that I know won't last more than half a generation. When I run wild, as they call it, it's my escape from the present. Not that I find any joy in my excesses. I'm up to my neck in the established order. . . .

¶ What is Tesman working on?

¶ *Hedda:* It's a book on the domestic industries of Brabant during the Middle Ages.

¶ I have to play the part of an idiot in order to be understood. Pretend that I want to rehabilitate myself in the eyes of the mob—today's mob.

¶ When I had finished with my latest book, I conceived the idea for a brilliant new work. You must help me with it. I need women, Hedda—! In the Middle Ages

[6] 1. But, my heavens, Tesm. was unmarried. *H.:* Yes, he was. *Th.:* But you married him. *H.:* Yes, I did. *Th.:* Then how can you say that . . . Well now—

2. But now he's married. *H.:* Yes, but not to someone else.

the female conscience was so constituted that if she discovered she had married her nephew, she was filled with rancor——

¶ Shouldn't the future strive for the great, the good, and the beautiful as Tesman says it should? Yes! But the great, the good, the beautiful of the future won't be the same as it is for us—

¶*H.:* I remember especially a red-headed girl whom I have seen on the street. *Br.:* I know whom you mean— *H.:* You called her—it was such a pretty name— *Br.:* I know her name too. But how do you know it was pretty? *H.:* Oh, Judge Brack, you are an idiot.

¶ The passenger and his trunk at the railway station. P. decides where he is going, buys his ticket. The trunk is attended to—

¶ Hedda: Slender figure of average height. Nobly shaped, aristocratic face with fine, wax-colored skin. The eyes have a veiled expression. Hair medium brown. Not especially abundant hair. Dressed in a loose-fitting dressing gown, white with blue trimmings. Composed and relaxed in her manners. The eyes steel-gray, almost lusterless.

¶ Mrs. Elvsted: weak build. The eyes round, rather prominent, almost as blue as water. Weak face with soft features. Nervous gestures, frightened expression—

¶ See above. E. L.'s idea of comradeship between man and woman. . . . The idea is a life-saver!

¶ If society won't let us live morally with them (women), then we'll have to live with them immorally—

¶*Tesman:* The new idea in E. L.'s book is that of progress resulting from the comradeship between man and woman.

¶ Hedda's basic demand is: I want to know everything, but keep myself clean.

¶ I want to know everything—everything—everything— *H.:*— —

H.: If only I could have lived like him!

¶ Is there something about Brabant? *B.:* What on earth is that? . . .

¶ The wager about the use of both pistols.

¶ *Miss T.:* Yes, this is the house of life and health. Now I shall go home to a house of sickness and death. God bless both of you. From now on I'll come out here every day to ask Bertha how things are—

¶ In the third act H. tells E. L. that she is not interested in the great questions—nor the great ideas—but in the great freedom of man. . . . But she hasn't the courage.

¶ The two ideals! *Tesman:* What in the name of God does he mean by that? What? What do we have to do with ideals?

¶ The new book treats of "the two ideals." Thea can give no information.

(6)

¶ NB! Brack had always thought that Hedda's short engagement to Tesman would come to nothing.

Hedda speaks of how she felt herself set aside, step by step, when her father was no longer in favor, when he retired and died without leaving anything. Then she realized, bitterly, that it was for his sake she had been made much of. And then she was already between twenty-five and twenty-six. In danger of becoming an old maid.

She thinks that in reality Tesman only feels a vain pride in having won her. His solicitude for her is the same as is shown for a thoroughbred horse or a valuable sporting dog. This, however, does not offend her. She merely regards it as a fact.

Hedda says to Brack that she does not think Tesman can be called ridiculous. But in reality she finds him so. Later on she finds him pitiable as well.

Tesman: Could you not call me by my Christian name?

Hedda: No, indeed I couldn't—unless they have given you some other name than the one you have.

Tesman puts Lövborg's manuscript in his pocket so that it may not be lost. Afterward it is Hedda who, by a casual remark, with tentative intention, gives him the idea of keeping it.

Then he reads it. A new line of thought is revealed to him. But the strain of the situation increases. Hedda awakens his jealousy.

¶ In the third act one thing after another comes to light about Lövborg's adventures in the course of the night. At last he comes himself, in quiet despair. "Where is the manuscript?" "Did I not leave it behind me here?" He does not know that he has done so.

But after all, of what use is the manuscript to him now! He is writing of the "moral doctrine of the future"! When he has just been released by the police!

¶ Hedda's despair is that there are doubtless so many chances of happiness in the world, but that she cannot discover them. It is the want of an object in life that torments her.

When Hedda beguiles T. into leading E. L. into ruin, it is done to test T.'s character.

¶ It is in Hedda's presence that the irresistible craving for excess always comes over E. L.

Tesman cannot understand that E. L. could wish to base his future on injury to another.

¶ *Hedda:* Do I hate T.? No, not at all. I only find him boring.

¶ *Brack:* But nobody else thinks so.

Hedda: Neither is there any one but myself who is married to him.

Brack: . . . not at all boring.

Hedda: Heavens, you always want me to express myself so correctly. Very well then, T. is not boring, but I am bored by living with him.

Hedda: . . . had no prospects. Well, perhaps you would have liked to see me in a convent (home for unmarried ladies).

Hedda: . . . then isn't it an honorable thing to profit by one's person? Don't actresses and others turn their advantages into profit. I had no other capital. Marriage —I thought it was like buying an annuity.

Hedda: Remember that I am the child of an old man —and a worn-out man too—or past his prime at any rate—perhaps that has left its mark.

Brack: Upon my word, I believe you have begun to brood over problems.

Hedda: Well, what cannot one take to doing when one has gone and got married.

(7)

¶ *E. L.:* It's impossible for me to call you Mrs. T. You will always be H. G. to me.

¶ Both Miss T. and B. have seen what lies in store for Hedda. . . . T. on the other hand cries out: My God, I had no idea.

¶ When E. L. tells H. that he cannot possibly confess
to Thea that her and his book has been lost, H. says:
I don't believe a word of that. *E.L.:* No, but I know how terribly dismayed she will be.

Translated by Evert Sprinchorn
(Section 6 translated by A. G. Chater)

THE PRIMACY OF CHARACTER[7]

Before I write down one word, I have to have the
character in mind through and through. I must penetrate
into the last wrinkle of his soul. I always proceed from the
individual; the stage setting, the dramatic ensemble, all
of that comes naturally and does not cause me any
worry, as soon as I am certain of the individual in every
aspect of his humanity. But I have to have his exterior
in mind also, down to the last button, how he stands and
walks, how he conducts himself, what his voice sounds like.
Then I do not let him go until his fate is fulfilled.

As a rule, I make three drafts of my dramas which
differ very much from each other in characterization,
not in action. When I proceed to the first sketch of
the material I feel as though I had the degree of ac-
quaintance with my characters that one acquires on a
railway journey; one has met and chatted about this or
that. With the next draft I see everything more clearly,
I know characters just about as one would know them
after a few weeks' stay in a spa; I have learned the
fundamental traits in their characters as well as their
little peculiarities; yet it is not impossible that I might
make an error in some essential matter. In the last draft,
finally, I stand at the limit of knowledge; I know my
people from close and long association—they are my
intimate friends, who will not disappoint me in any way;
in the manner in which I see them now, I shall always see
them.

[7] A. E. Zucker, *Ibsen: The Master Builder* (New York: Henry
Holt, 1929), pp. 194, 208. Copyright 1929, Henry Holt and
Company. Reprinted by permission of Henry Holt and Com-
pany.

AUGUST STRINDBERG
(1849-1912)

Miss Julie[1] (1888)

THEATRE HAS long seemed to me—in common with much other art—a *Biblia Pauperum*, a Bible in pictures for those who cannot read what is written or printed; and I see the playwright as a lay preacher peddling the ideas of his time in popular form, popular enough for the middle classes, mainstay of theatre audiences, to grasp the gist of the matter without troubling their brains too much. For this reason theatre has always been an elementary school for the young, the semieducated, and for women who still have a primitive capacity for deceiving themselves and letting themselves be deceived—who, that is to say, are susceptible to illusion and to suggestion from the author. I have therefore thought it not unlikely that in these days, when that rudimentary and immature thought process operating through fantasy appears to be developing into reflection, research, and analysis, that theatre, like religion, might be discarded as an outworn form for whose appreciation we lack the necessary conditions. This opinion is confirmed by the major crisis still prevailing in the theatres of Europe, and still more by the fact that in those countries of culture, producing the greatest thinkers of the age, namely England and Germany, drama—like other fine arts—is dead.

Some countries, it is true, have attempted to create a new drama by using the old forms with up-to-date contents, but not only has there been insufficient time for these new ideas to be popularized, so that the audience can grasp them, but also people have been so wrought up by the taking of sides that pure, disinterested appreciation has become impossible. One's deepest impressions are up-

---

1 August Strindberg, Author's foreword to *Miss Julie*, in *Six Plays of Strindberg*, translated by Elizabeth Sprigge (New York: Doubleday Anchor Books, 1955), *Miss Julie*, pp. 61–73; *A Dream Play*, p. 193. Copyright 1955 by Elizabeth Sprigge. Reprinted by permission of Willis Kingsley Wing.

set when an applauding or a hissing majority dominates
as forcefully and openly as it can in the theatre. Moreover,
as no new form has been devised for these new contents,
the new wine has burst the old bottles.

In this play I have not tried to do anything new, for
this cannot be done, but only to modernize the form to
meet the demands which may, I think, be made on this
art today. To this end I chose—or surrendered myself to—
a theme which claims to be outside the controversial
issues of today, since questions of social climbing or falling, of higher or lower, better or worse, of man and woman, are, have been, and will be of lasting interest. When I
took this theme from a true story told me some years ago,
which made a deep impression, I saw it as a subject for
tragedy, for as yet it is tragic to see one favored by
fortune go under, and still more to see a family heritage
die out, although a time may come when we have grown
so developed and enlightened that we shall view with
indifference life's spectacle, now seeming so brutal, cynical,
and heartless. Then we shall have dispensed with those
inferior, unreliable instruments of thought called feelings,
which become harmful and superfluous as reasoning
develops.

The fact that my heroine rouses pity is solely due to
weakness; we cannot resist fear of the same fate over-
taking us. The hypersensitive spectator may, it is true,
go beyond this kind of pity, while the man with belief in
the future may actually demand some suggestion for
remedying the evil—in other words some kind of policy.
But, to begin with, there is no such thing as absolute evil;
the downfall of one family is the good fortune of another,
which thereby gets a chance to rise, and, fortune being
only comparative, the alternation of rising and falling is
one of life's principal charms. Also, to the man of policy,
who wants to remedy the painful fact that the bird of
prey devours the dove, and lice the bird of prey, I should
like to put the question: why should it be remedied? Life
is not so mathematically idiotic as only to permit the big
to eat the small; it happens just as often that the bee kills
the lion or at least drives it mad.

That my tragedy depresses many people is their own
fault. When we have grown strong as the pioneers of the
French Revolution, we shall be happy and relieved to see
the national parks cleared of ancient rotting trees which